Perdita

Perdita

On Loss

Dylan Riley

VERSO

London • New York

First published by Verso 2024
© Dylan Riley 2024

1 3 5 7 9 10 8 6 4 2

Verso
UK: 6 Meard Street, London W1F 0EG
US: 388 Atlantic Avenue, Brooklyn, NY 11217
versobooks.com

Verso is the imprint of New Left Books

ISBN-13: 978-1-80429-608-0
ISBN-13: 978-1-80429-310-3 (UK EBK)
ISBN-13: 978-1-80429-611-0 (US EBK)

British Library Cataloguing in Publication Data
A catalogue record for this book is available from the British Library

Library of Congress Cataloging-in-Publication Data

Names: Riley, Dylan J., 1971- author.
Title: Perdita : on loss / Dylan Riley.
Description: London ; New York : Verso, 2024.
Identifiers: LCCN 2024019027 (print) | LCCN 2024019028 (ebook) | ISBN
9781804296080 (hardback) | ISBN 9781804296110 (ebook)
Subjects: LCSH: Riley, Dylan J., 1971- | Widowers—Biography. |
Bereavement—Psychological aspects | Loss (Psychology) |
Wives—Death—Psychological aspects. | Cancer—Patients—Family
relationships.
Classification: LCC BF575.G7 R54 2024 (print) | LCC BF575.G7 (ebook) |
DDC 155.9/37—dc23/eng/20240606
LC record available at https://lccn.loc.gov/2024019027
LC ebook record available at https://lccn.loc.gov/2024019028

Typeset in Fournier by MJ & N Gavan, Truro, Cornwall
Printed and bound by CPI Group (UK) Ltd, Croydon CR0 4YY

FSC
www.fsc.org
MIX
Paper | Supporting
responsible forestry
FSC® C171272

To Emanuela's circle, who helped me write this book and without whom I would be lost

Contents

Premessa

My Dearest Eamon,

I have written down these memories for you, the person I love more than anyone else in the world and for whom I would give my life a thousand times over. Although they are inevitably written from my point of view, I've tried as best I could to convey the feeling and flavor of what your mom was like and what we were like together. But in trying to explain what she meant to me, and how very deeply I loved her, I realized that I had to explain something about myself as well. In short, I had to explain the great losses, the *perdite*, that I have suffered. What I came to understand is that there is a connection among these losses in the sense that with each one, a door opened to something else. But that door had to be opened and the path beyond it taken. The passing of your mother imposes upon us a similar choice and responsibility. What are we to make of the fact that she existed, that she loved us, and that we in turn loved her? The truth is that the answer to that question is up to us. We must live in light of the fact that she did.

Parts of this text may be difficult or strange for you; they might seem like a betrayal or somehow indiscrete, as if you were looking in on private matters. Please read what you would like and skip what you don't want to. But I, for my part, did not want to knowingly keep any key elements from you. I am no saint, and I loved your mother passionately, not platonically. Our marriage was, from any conventional point of view, wildly implausible; and you, my dear son, are the miraculous product of this beautiful, rather crazy, and all-too-brief love affair.

Love,
Dad

Prefazione

I wanted the world to know what it had lost and maybe, in knowing it, to make her live again in that knowledge. Loss is a completely generic human experience, but, like life itself, each instance is doubly specific because it is linked to both a particular person and a particular connection to that person. This is the reality that escapes the genre of advice literature, even though every such volume contains one version or another of the phrase "every loss is unique." That is not to say that one does not learn from reading about the losses of others, but the lessons are as much negative as positive; they allow one, more properly, to specify the particularity of one's own grief. Accordingly, this little volume offers no advice. It tries, more simply, to represent a particular lost connection.

The text is composed in three parts organized around four losses. The first part, *Prima* (before), comprises scenes imposed by my parents' divorce and the move from the house where I had my first memories, as well as the loss of my first two loves. The second is called *Noi* (us) and contains everything that I could render about the life I had with Emanuela—a life that lasted twenty-four years from when I met her in August 1998 to when she passed away in January 2022. The third one is called *Dopo* (after). It describes mostly internal states, and its reflective and expressive tone differs from the first two.

The writing moves at different rhythms. Some of the prose covers years in just a few lines; some dwells on specific scenes. Wherever possible, I have tried to link my thoughts to a particular image, to make what was happening palpable.

Much of the writing, especially in the last part of the book, first appeared as blog posts on a site that Emanuela had set up to organize help from our friends. In the months immediately following her passing, I continued to post on it, partly as a way of trying to hold on to her by holding together the community that she had created. It is my hope that by arranging these posts in a volume, I can somehow render them more permanent and public.

The period in which I wrote this book, that few months of disorienting anguish that immediately follows a great loss, is now closed. My position in the world, my hopes and fears, the peculiar nature of my project, is now slightly clearer. So, the journey continues, but to some new destination, one unimaginable just three years before. If there is one thing I would like to convey, it is the fundamental openness and contingency of human existence, the internal connections among ephemerality, freedom, grief, loss, and history. We human beings are doomed to ride the arrow of time for just a moment, and everything we do, including our many efforts to struggle against this central fact, unfolds within its context. This is not to embrace some gloomy existential outlook about "living toward death" but rather to recognize that hope itself, that tricky and dangerous emotion, grows out of the soil of our mortality, and of the mortality of those we love.

Prima

Deerwood

There was Richard Fogel and his family; they lived one or two houses down from us. Hill people who had relocated to Louisville for mysterious reasons. Richard, who must have been in his very early twenties, was thin as a rail, had dark hair and a mustache somewhat like my dad. I remember him in mustard-colored shirts and brown pants. He had sad, furtive eyes and would spend hours at our house poring over maps of anything—maps of Kentucky, maps of the US, maps of the world. He loved them but had none at home. I remember seeing his parents only once or twice; they seemed unimaginably old and grumpy. I don't recall him saying more than two words: a mumbled thanks to my father. Did they drink Falls City Beer together on the screened-in porch out back? It's possible, but Richard may have been too young.

There were the Marks: the good one and the bad one. The good Mark lived directly across the street from us in a house painted red and white like a candy cane, with a yard full of bleached gravel and an impressive assortment of ceramic animals and gnomes. My brother and I were especially envious of the good Mark because he had what we did not: a huge collection of toy guns. There were pistols and M16 rifles, munition boxes, ammo belts, and even a toy flamethrower. All this was collected in a giant chest in his room. Control over this fundamental resource gave him an almost godlike status in the neighborhood. The good Mark determined and armed the "teams" when we played war, which we did almost constantly. (We, by contrast, were allowed only guns of "historic value." I guess this was mom's compromise with juvenile militarism, the violence of settler colonialism being somehow more acceptable and edifying than that of World

War II, Vietnam, or Korea; I had a colonial-era pistol cap-gun and my brother a long rifle: weapons which rendered us ridiculous in the conflict against the M16 and the flamethrower, and thus the need to borrow from the good Mark.)

The bad Mark lived down the street on our side; he was older. We never went inside his house; it was always dark, and there was a feeling of violence about the place. Sometimes, I think, he played with us; but more often he was simply a menacing presence, a threat. I had played with his little brother one day, but he stole all my Hot Wheels. He tricked me by putting them in his yellow Tonka truck. I even helped him do it; after this breach of trust, we could never be friends.

One day the bad Mark shot the good Mark with a BB gun just below his eye and was taken away in a police car. He had supposedly lain in wait for hours among the garden gnomes for the good Mark to appear. I remember seeing his face looking out, forlorn, from the back of the cruiser, and thinking he probably only wanted to be the good Mark. Perhaps he thought if he could just eliminate his rival, the rest of the neighborhood would rally to him, and he would be able to decide the teams.

There was Jeff Green, the Black kid. He lived on our side too. His family had a Chihuahua that barked hysterically every time we came to the door. I remember his kitchen, which was the color of Benedictine dip; somehow I always associated this kitchen with his name. Jeff, who was good at baseball, was always perfectly dressed, as was his mother. I don't remember meeting his father. The days were long and friend filled and sunny and above all, apart from the menace of the bad Mark, without worry.

Space Beer

It must have been in the late spring or early summer. My mom was in the kitchen, and our transistor radio with a single speaker and a broken antenna was blaring out Glen Campbell's "Like a Rhinestone Cowboy." I was thinking of my dad's words as I looked at the brown boxes of sour-smelling, empty longnecks stacked neatly on the screened-in back porch and printed with the red "Falls City Beer" label. "Falls City Beer is about the best damned beer there is, not like that horse-piss-in-a-bottle Budweiser." I think I sensed, even then, an element of fraternal competition in Dad's words: Uncle Bill was a dedicated Bud man, and Dad disdained most of the things that he liked. I certainly couldn't tell the difference. To me, all beer looked, smelled, and tasted very much like what I imagined horse piss to be.

Dad's beer mugs, however, were cool. There was the rounded pewter one with a dent in it that somehow, years later, ended its life in the humiliating position of a dog-food scoop. There was the copper one, in which everything tasted strange. And then there was the one with glass at the bottom. "Dad, why does it have a glass bottom?"

"It's called a Jesse James mug; the glass's so when you're drinking your beer you can look through and see if somebody tries to pull a gun on you and you shoot first."

The mugs were for beer; no Coke or Kool-Aid was allowed to touch them. That's when I hit upon it; I would make my own beer, except mine would be tasty. I even had a name: space beer. What was beer made of? It seemed like a weird, spicy version of ginger ale; so I pulled as many things as I could think of from the spice cabinet (black pepper, ginger powder, mustard powder, chili flakes, sage) and, for good measure, tore up a big wad of grass. I took the pewter mug, threw the ingredients together, and poured my mom's "Canada Dry" over them; the concoction fizzed and popped. "Space beer!" I exclaimed, and I drank to the dregs.

Goodbye

A yellow vinyl pull-down shade covered one side of the tall wooden front door. Mom had cut circular holes in it at varying heights so that we could look out down the stairs to the street beyond. We could see the good Mark's house, and then to the right of it an alley, and the bank; this last building fascinated me because it had a real vault, visible from the green-carpeted lobby where tellers spoke in soft voices and money changed hands. The door was a huge, thick, round steel thing that opened outward to reveal a set of bars. An orangish yellow glow emanated from there, and I imagined that it contained an enormous stash of gold.

Sometimes Dad and I would sit on the steps and watch the chimney sweeps circle around the bank. "Cigars with wings," he would say. We also looked out for passing cars. The heterogeneity of the rolling stock was greater then, and trucks from the forties and early fifties would still occasionally pass by as well as these: the infamous Ford Pinto that supposedly exploded at the slightest rear impact; the AMC Gremlin; something from Renault called Le Car, an attempt by the French to enter the US market. There were many Fiats as well; indeed, until the late seventies these still occupied the subcompact niche. Our family had one. Japanese imports were already becoming more common, but the earliest ones were of questionable quality. There was the awful Datsun B210, one of which my uncle owned and, like Budweiser, was an object of my dad's derision. Volkswagens, of course, were everywhere, together with Chevrolet Chevelles, DeVilles, and

Bel Airs, and various other enormous American models, each of which had some vaguely "continental"-sounding name.

What interested me most, however, when I was very small, was not the make or model but the wheels; to my mind there were two basic categories: those with hubcaps and those without, which I called "eeny-weenies," and which excited me very much for some reason. I remember sitting on the front porch and shouting when a hubcap-less car passed, "Eeny-weenie! Eeny-weenie!" Dad would laugh and hold me in his lap, and we would make a game of counting how many we saw.

It was late summer or early fall; Dad was leaving for a place called "New Orleans." I remember wondering what was new about it, and what the old one was like. I looked up at him as he stood by the door. He was still very young; his mustachioed face, slim frame, and leather cowboy hat gave him a raffish air. He looked very ready to leave, and I had some feeling that his connection to us was tenuous. He was forever going somewhere on his motorcycle: working, or socializing. There was always an air of frenetic activity about him: some project or other that had to be done but seldom seemed to include us, or only contingently so. The best way to spend time with Dad was to join him in our dank basement when he was engaged in drilling or sawing.

He had devised an elaborate system for storing his screws by nailing the lids of baby food jars to a beam in the ceiling. The jars were thereby suspended for easy access, the screws themselves arranged in order of size along the beam. I did a lot of holding of pieces of wood and tools; I learned the difference between a two-by-four and a four-by-four; I knew what a post-hole digger was, and an entrenching tool. Sometimes I would get bored and crawl off into a musty corner to play in the dirt with my Hot Wheels or army men. It was enough just to be around him.

There was the shouting too, mostly from Mom. Things about responsibility, and "You have children." I didn't really follow along. I had heard the word "divorce" before; it was terrifying and inconceivable, like "death" or "outer space." But it seemed relevant now, with him on the doorstep looking so eager to be out. "Dad, you're not going to divorce us, are you?" I had no clear idea what exactly my question meant.

He laughed and took me in his arms: "No, we're all going to New Orleans. I just have to get some things set up down there."

Mom was irritable, as she often was then. Where was Dad? He had been gone a long time. We had even had to move, leaving all our friends behind on Deerwood and taking up residence in Seneca Gardens at my grandparents' old house. It was boring, and the kids all looked the same. No more playing war; it was all basketball and football and driving around everywhere. We were turning onto the street before our house. "When's Dad coming home?" I asked.

"He's not coming home, Dylan. We're getting a divorce." The sadness came over me in an enormous black wave, and I sobbed uncontrollably for hours. I had learned for the first time the meaning of loss.

Middle School

The two of them formed a pair: there was a brunette one and a blonde one. I was interested in the blonde one. It must have been sixth grade, and I was seated at a round faux-wood table on one of the bright orange chairs with chrome plated legs made of tubular steel. They were seated on the other side of the room and had all the accoutrements of well-put-together girlhood: comfortable-looking clothes, little leather moccasin-like shoes, and the inevitable Trapper Keeper—a brightly colored binder from which they extracted clean and flat sheets of paper and well-done homework assignments.

I had on Toughskins (Sears's answer to Levi's, made from some indestructible synthetic-fabric-and-denim blend), which had once been hemmed but were now let out, giving them the telltale "coffee-can" look, and a plaid shirt a couple sizes too small. My binder was a damaged hand-me-down from my brother, and my homework looked as it if it had been slightly chewed. I was trying to look at the blonde one in a way that wouldn't draw attention to myself, which meant that I ended up staring at the brunette.

At the end of class, Amy, the blonde one, piped up from across the room, loud enough for everyone to hear: "Why are you making eyes at Kim? You should take a picture. It would last longer!" Amid the general hilarity, my humiliation was complete. I felt myself turning completely red and scurried out of class as fast as I could. The disaster was total. Not only had I been outed as an ogler; she had totally misunderstood whom I was interested in. But maybe in the end that was better. In any case, I regarded her as unattainable, and I thought it likely that she placed me somewhere between a snail and slug in the great chain of middle school being.

Rooftop

It was a sticky summer evening, but clear enough that some stars could be seen twinkling through the humid air. Above the two added-on attic bedrooms, the roof was completely flat, and this is where we were lying, looking up at the sky. Amy grabbed my hand tightly. The chasm that had separated us just a couple of years before had now narrowed to nothing. I felt an electric pulse course through my body. It wasn't desire as an adult might experience but rather a giddy, slightly terrifying sensation, like being at the top of a roller coaster hill before the plunge.

She turned to face me; we kissed. She was doing something with her tongue that felt both surprising and thrilling. We passed the next hour or so exploring this activity and doing a lot of rolling around. When we returned to our friends below, both of us were covered with tar smudges.

Correspondents

Amy left for college about a month before I did. Typical for us, we had never had a straightforward conversation about what this meant. In the interlude I pursued a crush that I had carried around in a state of latency for years. From the autumn of 1983 to the summer of 1984 I lived in a small town north of Dundee called Carnoustie, Scotland, because my mother had secured a teacher exchange position through the Fulbright Program.

Gray-eyed and high-cheekboned Sophie had written me letters during my year there: dozens of them. The paper on which these missives were inscribed varied in color and shape, sometimes blue or pink, sometimes heart shaped, or square, or lined. She never used airmail envelopes and was extravagant with her stamps. The messages were carefully produced with her small-lettered but neat handwriting, their content touchingly quotidian. Descriptions of pets loomed large.

After I returned to Louisville—I was thirteen at the time—we had even gone on what I had supposed was a date to see the Alfred Hitchcock film *Rope*. But there was some barrier between us. She had very definite views on a wide variety of subjects that seemed idiosyncratic: for example, veganism, which was an oddity at that time and place; and an antipathy to Sophia Loren, whom I always found to be very striking. At the time I couldn't understand that this expressed an intellectual personality at once rooted (she was, after all, very much a "Louisvillian") and highly sophisticated; she had quite precocious taste in books and films, presumably in part because her father owned a bookstore that functioned as a sort of local salon. She also played the violin, like I did. Her instrument's case was festooned with stickers of every sort. There were animals and rainbows; some were puffy, others flat. One I remembered very clearly. It said, "Women belong in the House . . . and in the Senate," which I found clever. Stickers were also the currency of her friendship. She carried sheets of them around in her backpack and would sometimes give some to me. I treasured them, though rather secretively.

There was also the time—it must have been the summer of my sixth-grade year—when we went on a school trip to Camp Piomingo, a YMCA facility just outside of Louisville on a bend of the Ohio River. One of the activities was a night walk. As we tramped along the path, shrouded in darkness and surrounded by our classmates, our hands found one another and clasped. At the end of the walk, we reached a clearing where we lay down and looked up at the dimly twinkling stars that were just bright enough to pierce the steamy air of the Kentucky summer. It had been thrilling but was without immediate sequel.

Ambiguous flirtation would continue off and on, especially in English class, when she had been a senior and I a junior. But nothing would happen until that final summer when, for a blissful couple of weeks, we tried what had been frustrated for so many years. But I left, and we fell entirely out of contact. She always existed for me as a counterfactual, somehow laminated onto the internal skin of my emotional existence, a suppressed possibility partially constitutive, as are all objective absences, of who I became.

Endings

The end was full of miscommunication and pain. Once I arrived in New York to attend Eugene Lang College at the New School, the period of late-summer ambiguity seemed to pass, and Amy and I fell back together again. Characteristically, nothing was said; it simply happened. She visited, I visited. Many times during that first year, I would wait anxiously on the platform of Grand Central Terminal for the arrival of the train from Poughkeepsie. Seeing her emerge with her laughing eyes and golden hair, my heart would leap; we could pretend, at least for a couple of nights, to be together—but now in Manhattan rather than the oppressive provincialism of Louisville, with all its wagging tongues, expectations, and judgments.

We would go to museums, to restaurants and bars we could not afford; we would pretend to be, in short, what we certainly were not: adults in the city. It was impassioned but also relentlessly poignant, the two things in a way reinforcing one another. She was stunningly beautiful, we were achingly in love, but so much seemed to conspire against us, including geography: we had chosen different colleges, although ones that were close enough that we could just maintain something like a romance. But there were other matters—for example, my room.

When she came to New York those first few times, intimacy had to be negotiated with my roommate: a boorish idiot from Boston whose main ambition in life seemed to be to get high on nitrous oxide canisters and loudly screw his girlfriend in semi-public. But we were stubborn. One time we even considered getting a room at the Roosevelt Hotel, where Emanuela would later stay when she visited with her friends Mario and Patrizia in 1998. (It was quite outside our budget at the time.) The objective situation constantly pulled us apart. We resisted. During the summer after that first year, we hatched a scheme together to achieve the cohabitation that was our constantly thwarted ambition. Amy arranged to stay at Bard, where she was going to college, for a few weeks into the summer and had found us both jobs working at an antique show loading and unloading cumbersome and delicate furniture from vehicles that always seemed far too small; the vendors would arrive in modestly sized trucks and cars from which massive armoires, grandfather clocks, and tables protruded at odd angles, precariously held in place by ropes and bungies and swaddled in moving blankets.

I learned how to move furniture, a skill that did not come naturally. If there was a difficult and awkward way to move something, or in general to achieve some physical result, I always lit upon that first. But during that summer I reasonably quickly got the hang of how to use angles and weight to my advantage. We worked like mules and enjoyed it. At some point I also washed dishes at a local diner. The place was wooden and deep red with a small, dingy kitchen featuring an oven whose insides were coated in a thick layer of carbonized detritus.

My boss, and the restaurant's cook, was a taciturn man, probably in his late sixties, who I assumed was the owner. We shuffled around in a silent dance during the lunch rushes, one dirtying dishes, the other washing them. The man seemed impressed by my dedication, and we began to chat about this and that. At the end of my shifts I returned to Bard bone tired, my clothes permeated by the sour smell of slightly spoiled dairy that always accompanies the dishwasher.

It was a blissful month or so; Amy and I could sleep together in the same bed unmolested and unjudged. We were free, for that brief moment, from all the burdens and obstacles, the endless family commitments, the silent expectations, the constant whispering, "But they're so young." What no one seemed to understand about us was how much we gave, or tried to give, to one another. We had been each other's guide and role model, therapist and confidante. We explored our bodies together, and our souls as well. Our intimacy was bottomless; we could not imagine being apart, despite a future that seemed anything but assured.

As the early summer slipped toward the solstice, we left upstate New York and headed west, first returning to Louisville and then striking out on the road trip with our good friend Matt in his small truck. The trip across the vast continent was tiring, uncomfortable, and cramped. But I was happy just to be beside her and would have traversed the globe a dozen times in that little cab if only to hold on to that; of course, I was too foolish and tongue tied to tell her anything so true, but maybe she felt it.

The apartment in San Francisco was a rather miserable disappointment for us both: gray, dirty, dark, with shag carpet and dreary blue walls permeated by the faint smell of beer. We sought employment and somehow ended up canvasing for a Ralph Nader–sponsored public auto-insurance ballot initiative: "Voter Revolt" was splashed everywhere in the neon-lit office where our vaguely Redfordesque leader and his impressively fit lesbian sidekick with the long black hair would give us pep talks and advice about how to collect signatures and donations. It all seemed so easy in that office in the Flood Building.

The reality of the suburbs just on the other side of the Caldecott Tunnel, crawling in the early nineties with rock-ribbed

Republicans, libertarians of various and sundry hues, and even the occasional John Bircher, was quite different. The electoral verities of the Golden State ground down our modest ambition to earn a living wage; after all, we worked on commission, tramping hopelessly around the suburbs subjected to an alternating barrage of hostile dogs and discourses on the dangers of socialism from ruddy-faced and dour men whose whole social being conspired, however implausibly in that great land of public works, to convince them that they were entirely self-made.

Those suburban neo-peasants, a sack of potatoes if there ever was one, considered themselves exemplars of individual initiative and the embodiment of freedom against the dangers of collectivism, even as they drove on federal highways and tended their thirsty lawns with municipally provided water—the product of a hydraulic system whose ambition and extent would have shamed the pharaohs. The work, in short, was hopeless.

Our desire for a summer together petered out in a meaningless and fruitless routine. She left; I stayed. We made love the night before she returned home with an intensity heightened by the sad foreboding that this was an ending. After her departure, I was lonely beyond words; but a callous started to form around my emotional wound. I found another job, the fourth that summer. This time it was at the Klein Deli on Potrero Hill: the neighborhood was still somewhat affordable. I stocked the shelves, made sandwiches, and washed enormous white tubs that had once held mayonnaise, the remnants of which would float about on the gray dishwater like massive cottage cheese curds or marshmallows—something I found particularly revolting. Toward the end of the summer, my mother brought me back to Louisville, where I felt defeated and weak. Amy's dalliances, real and suspected, drove me crazy with feelings of jealousy and betrayal. I wanted to react in kind, to hurt her like she was hurting me. But I could not. Our romance lingered on somehow into the fall and winter like some mortally wounded animal slowly yielding to its fate. Too much anger, too little time, too many implacable facts against us. The miracle was always not that it collapsed but that it had lasted as long as it did. This was the second great loss.

Artist

We had a class together, on European history, I think. The instructor, Carroll Joynes, was a soft-spoken, charming, and well-appointed Chicago guy. The classroom was simple, almost austere, as were most at Eugene Lang College. A row of windows opposite the door overlooked Twelfth Street. The chairs were arranged in a rough horseshoe. As one entered the room, Professor Joynes sat behind a desk to the right. I remember three things from the content of the class: a discussion of Polybius's theory of history, Joynes telling us that Aristotle was a "very smart man," and Max Weber's "Social Causes of the Decline of Ancient Civilization," the essay, together with Perry Anderson's *Passages from Antiquity to Feudalism*, that made me want to become a sociologist.

Mostly, however, I remember the people. There was a large-headed, sad-eyed teaching assistant, a PhD in philosophy, also from Chicago, who was very friendly and intelligent but somewhat melancholy. He liked to talk about Leo Strauss and poked fun at my enthusiasm for structural Marxism—especially Nicos Poulantzas. I remember Stephanie and Sam. I sat near the windows, they sat next to one another on the opposite side near the door. Sam was tall and elegant and quite beautiful, with dark hair and deep brown eyes.

One evening we got smashingly drunk together on the Lower East Side and ended up at her apartment, where nothing much happened. The next morning, I made her a plate of eggs, we had coffee, and that was it. Somehow, Sam always seemed like a reserved older sister, even though we must all have been roughly the same age.

Stephanie, in contrast, was a whirling chaos of creative energy. She was laughter and gray eyes and curiosity and intelligence, surrounded by a little electrical field of excitement. There was also the stuff: bags and papers stained with coffee and paint and projects in various stages of completion. Sometimes she cast a glance over at me, or so I imagined, with those striking eyes, and I felt a thrill.

Nothing happened between us in the class; but after it had finished, we ran into one another at a bar on Sixth Street between avenues C and D. It must have been early 1991. It was certainly cold. The place had a large plate-glass window that faced the street. The bar itself was to the left as one entered. In the center of the room were tables and chairs; and along the wall to the right were booths upholstered in Naugahyde. In the back, away from the street, was a pool table and a jukebox from which Johnny Cash and Dwight Yoakam seemed always to be twanging. I was there with Anthony, my roommate and friend, an Italian American guy whose grandmother lived in Queens and whose father had been assassinated in some mob hit and therefore, when he was ten or twelve, had had to decamp to an arid suburb of Columbus, Ohio, with his mother. We were drinking beer and complaining about our other housemate, who we agreed was behaving like a needy and jilted lover. My mood was generally glum. Whatever I had with Amy was over, and my living situation was far from ideal.

At that moment, the improbable pair burst through the door, Sandra (a flamboyant rich girl from New Jersey) and Stephanie. Their energy, especially Stephanie's, electrified the place, turning it from a dreary East Side watering hole into a little cabaret. It was as if the room had suddenly been festooned with Christmas lights. I think it was Stephanie who came and asked to join us, or maybe I asked her. She wore red lipstick, a colorful hat, and a leather jacket with fringes that at some point during the evening that followed became stained with white paint.

The two of them must have been out on the town, although it was most definitely a weekday. I had never quite seen her like this; she was very fetching. We drank; we talked about being Southerners; we laughed; we put on Cash's "Ring of Fire" and started to play pool. I was relatively good at it, having learned with my brothers over many Alabama summers when we were left to entertain ourselves while Dad worked. We formed teams that conveniently adumbrated couples: it was the Southerners against the Yankees. At some point the four of us left the bar and piled into to Sandra's SUV (these were still a novelty in the early nineties). At some point Stephanie and I were kissing one another; at some point we were holding hands; at some point were saying goodbye outside her place in Williamsburg, the white one with the crooked floors and the great light. That evening I had stumbled through a portal; I was part of Stephanie's world now, and I liked it very much.

Hammond

The house was one of those huge old Gulf Coast places with a giant tree in the front lawn and a massive porch. The downstairs was open with dark wood everywhere and mercifully well air-conditioned. Stephanie's mom was fluttering about the kitchen, which I remember as being very bright and very yellow. Her father, upright (although not particularly tall), fit, and handsome despite, or because, of his receding hairline scrutinized me rather severely while shaking my hand, in what felt more like a test than a gesture of welcome. There was a dinner; I think grace was said. My conversational strategy was to demonstrate unreserved enthusiasm for everything connected to Louisiana, and particularly their house, in the hopes that more dangerous topics, especially politics, might be avoided.

Stephanie seemed at once both very close to, and very distant from, her parents. It was the return of the black sheep and the princess, all bound up in one person. I remember watching her talk to her father and noticing the uncanny similarities of gesture and comportment, above all the way they laughed. But there was also an electric tension between them that I could imagine breaking out in a clap of thunder and lightning at any moment.

Then there was her bedroom. It was on the second floor. One had to cross a TV area littered with her brothers' sports equipment. The room seemed to recapitulate in life size the dollhouse that was prominently displayed within it. The walls were covered with the repeating pattern of a wedding bouquet. Pillows and pink things were arranged carefully on a bed that seemed to be so thoroughly made it would occur to no one to try to sleep in it. Above all the place seemed to have absolutely no connection with the person I knew her to be. It was as if her mother (I supposed it was mainly her project) had constructed an elaborate shrine to an imaginary daughter. Not that I hadn't seen "girls' rooms" like this before back in Kentucky; Stephanie's, however, was a virtuosic example. Such spaces seemed, among other things, designed to ward off the threat of sexual activity.

Potential lovers would presumably wither under the assault of the cloying cuteness that oozed out from every nook and cranny.

Stephanie burst into laughter. "Here's my room, Dyl," she said. I loved her very, very much. We had been together six months or so. Those gray eyes and sandy hair, her broad smile and easy laugh. She was all chaos and energy, the product of the contradictory poles that made up her personality: somewhat macho and extremely feminine, daddy's girl and rebel, uncompromising artist with a taste for highly sweetened Starbucks concoctions and daiquiris, naive Southerner and hard-boiled denizen of Williamsburg, gourmand who didn't know what a peppercorn was. It was as if these opposite impulses had created a whirling emotional dynamo so that being around her always felt slightly thrilling and dangerous, even when we were engaged in the most mundane activities.

There was also the fact that she was one of the very few people outside my family and my closest friends to call me "Dyl," and it came to her so naturally. Eventually all that energy would tear us apart; basically, I was too bookish and reserved, and when the outlet of the university had been removed with the move to Chicago, our personalities proved incompatible. But in that moment, she was the entire world to me, and I would have thrown myself off a cliff for her.

We spent most of the rest of our stay there in her studio, which might better have been described as a refuge: a room above the garage set off from the main house. There we painted, drank (mostly daiquiris and Abita beers), and generally wallowed in a state of blissful dissipation.

We took a couple of trips in her car, an old red Honda Prelude (a gift from her dad?). First, there was a trip to New Orleans during which we stopped to eat boudin, a spicy sausage with rice and pork, at a little stand somewhere along Interstate 55. Then there was a longer jaunt out on the Delta. Our idea was to drive as far south as possible, but we didn't reach Venice. On the way, we passed a moldering two-story wood-framed place with a deep wraparound porch. A tumbled-down shed stood off to the side. At first glance, the old mansion looked abandoned, and Stephanie leapt out of the car to explore in her usual insouciant manner; I think I hung back a bit, as there was something slightly menacing about it. As we approached the porch, we both pulled up short at a handwritten sign hanging on one of the blanket-curtained French doors reading: "Don't wake. Day sleeper." As fast as the carolers escaping the old woman singing "Good King Wenceslas" in *A Child's Christmas in Wales*, we piled into the car and were gone. In short, the whole experience was heavenly.

Chicago

What we had petered out in a gray anti-climax, then lingered on as quasi-intimacy for a year or so. It's hard to identify a key turning point: we never fought, or at least I don't remember ever fighting. (Perhaps that was part of the problem). There were definite signs, however. The summer before the move to Chicago, Stephanie had gone to the Chautauqua Institution to attend a painting retreat of some kind. We talked on the phone often, but she seemed distant. I was in Louisville when she called the last time before coming back to New York. "Dyl, I have to tell you something," she said. "I slept with a guy here." I was deeply hurt, but I couldn't muster any outrage.

We had a very strange conversation after that. I asked her if she wanted to leave me, but she somehow shifted the impetus, asking if I wanted her to come back home. I said something to the effect of "Of course I do." I got the feeling, even then, that what she really wanted from me was anger: a blow-up fight ending in some kind of dramatic statement; in short, she wanted a breakup, but initiated by me. That, I think, would have made life easier for her. Then there was the strange business about the roommate who stayed with us (Stephanie and I had rented an apartment in Williamsburg together with my close friend from Louisville, Josh Hines) during her time at the retreat. Somehow, I didn't know until later that he was an ex-boyfriend of some sort, and he never washed the dishes. I resented that she introduced this person into our apartment, although, wrongly, I kept this to myself. Already before the move to Chicago, then, there were festering wounds that had been only lightly plastered over and were poisoning us.

The apartment she had found in the Pilsen neighborhood during the fall of 1993 was cavernous. There was some kind of blue-green or grayish green paint (its ambiguous and transitional character a portent), and a substantial kitchen. I also remember a massive wooden table where I would work. My mother had previously decided to dump on us a bunch of furniture made of dark, heavy wood, which would make what was to come unnecessarily expensive and painful. But basic things were missing; there was no door on the bathroom, for example. The neighborhood was also substantially worse than Williamsburg; I remember one evening when we heard shots outside the window. They were close enough that following each, we could make out the "clink" as the bullet case fell to the ground.

It was clear that Chicago was Stephanie's gig; she wanted to be there to get into set design as it was a more innovative and approachable scene than anything available in New York. I tried to figure things out: I strung together a couple of jobs, one as the administrative assistant of a very demanding woman from Lincoln Park with whom Stephanie put me in touch, and another working at the box office of the Steppenwolf Theatre Company. But none of it made much sense for me. It was easy enough to find entry-level work in New York City; why was I here? The answer was obvious: for her. But she was clearly feeling suffocated by me.

She spent long hours working on her theater projects, and she had a job at a nightclub that made me jealous. I began to feel like a useless appendage, a dreary obligation that pulled Stephanie away from things in which she was truly interested. This was self-fulfilling; I was turning into one of those glum partners whose melancholic self-absorption drives people away. I'm sure that I became sullen and unpleasant, and we began, as the expression goes, to "drift apart." I was growing to dislike myself and could hardly blame her if she was losing interest.

We were laying in our improvised bedroom, while the light from the streetlamp outside splashed over the blue-green walls. Desire had drained out of both of us; we played the role of nothing more than human comforters for one another. She looked at me and said, "Dyl, I can't do this anymore." I knew, and was frankly relieved. Perhaps it was weakness on my part that I hadn't tried to end things earlier, or even that I had come to Chicago at all. Why had I put this on her? She was trying to have her life, and what exactly was I doing there? And here we were surrounded by my mother's furniture. It was a weird ending.

There was a brief coda, a period in which we were living together but were no longer a couple. Ian and Hallie, her friends from New York who had preceded her in the move, were also going through some kind of rough patch at that point. I remember spending a lot of time drinking with Ian in various Chicago bars. At one point he was trying to set me up with a very pleasant and attractive blonde woman who was friends with his current love interest, but for whom I could muster no enthusiasm. I left Chicago soon after that, early spring of 1994.

Stephanie and I had to drive all my mother's furniture back down to Louisville in a U-Haul; we said our goodbyes, and I remember looking out the front window and seeing her drive away. I don't know what I felt then; tears, certainly, but also a flat sense of inevitability about the whole thing. My decision to move to Chicago had not been a good one. But then again, how could I not have gone? The key point is that I deeply loved Stephanie, and the idea of not going never really occurred to me.

Strangely, we grew closer again after I left. When I first moved out to California, we would talk for hours on the phone. I was extremely lonely in those early months living with my father and Jessica, my stepmother (they had moved to the Golden State in 1991), and feeling close to a complete failure; but it was clear also that she needed me for something. Our connection continued even to the early period of my time at the University of California, Los Angeles, where I had gone to study sociology.

The last time we were together was on a visit to Chicago; it must have been in 1995 or 1996. Stephanie had moved into a high-ceilinged place with an open floor plan. When I saw her, it was if we had never been apart; we spent an intense weekend together, talking late into the night; our intimacy had returned. It was as if, for that brief moment, the dreary interlude with the blue-green or gray-green apartment had never happened. I have not seen her since. But I think about her often, and what we had together is a crucial piece of the mosaic of my personality. Losing what we had was the third great loss of my life.

Hollywood

The place I first had in Los Angeles was a room in a house perched on the Hollywood Hills. These last loom over Sunset Boulevard, and are studded with implausibly positioned structures, half of which seem like they are about to slide off the fragile slopes and crash into the river of cars below. It was near the Chateau Marmont, a haunt steeped in Hollywood lore: overdoses, betrayals, even talk of a murder. The building I lived in, which must have been from the twenties, was all turrets and white plaster trimmed with dark wood. The proprietors were an elderly Jewish couple; I recalled thinking them a bit overfond of Israel and NATO, but understandably so given their "ethnicity" and generation. I had to interview for the "opportunity" to rent the room. It helped that the couple was convinced that I was Jewish, and, while false, I did nothing to disabuse them of this notion.

They were nice enough, if a bit invasive. My room was on the northeast corner and had two entrances: one that led to the kitchen, and another with a set of French doors that opened directly onto a little patio with two chaises longues, which sat in a sort of well surrounded by a garden that stretched up the hill in back of the house. Amy had come over for dinner, or perhaps we had gone out. We were now reclining on the chaises longues looking up at the branches of an oak that stretched over the patio and enjoying the balmy air of the LA evening. We were remembering.

She was as striking as ever with her golden hair, gray-green eyes, and bronze skin. That night she seemed particularly put together; dressed impeccably and exuding the confidence of early adulthood. There was talk of a job that sounded impressive, but which I didn't quite understand. There were mentions of travel to exotic places with her boyfriend, an Argentinian, although I distinctly heard her use the past tense in relation to this person. We were so comfortable together, exchanging memories: high school, parents, siblings, above all so many shared experiences. (After all, we were both still very young, in our early twenties, and these recollections were not so far off.) A lull opened in the conversation. I approached the question in an indirect and defensive way, placing myself outside and above the moment, shifting as much of the responsibility to her as possible. This had always been my way, a character flaw perhaps. "Have you ever thought about us getting back together?" I asked. If she was caught off guard, there was no hint of it in her beautiful face, which was as relaxed and confident as ever. "No. I'm sure I don't want that," she answered.

The casual finality of her reply brooked no response. We chatted for a bit more, then parted amicably. I hoped I had not ruined the evening with my maladroitness. Later, as I was washing our glasses in the sink, I laughed to myself. What had I been thinking? Our paths were very different now, however much we may have loved each other as teenagers (and I was convinced that we had loved each other about as much as teenagers are capable). She, who always had a greater sense of realism than I, and in any case was quite obviously still in love with the handsome Argentinian (even if there was something ambiguous and nonfinal about that relationship), had been, as usual, absolutely right. After that, although we saw each other a few more times in LA, where she lived for a time, it was clear our lives were moving on different tracks. I grew to love this strange city, if one can call it that, and threw myself into my work with a ferocious intensity that sometimes terrified my friends from before. Then, after a few years, I met Emanuela in that old building on Via Genova.

City of Angels

Among the many things I learned in Los Angeles, one of the most important was how to be alone. From my early teens to my early twenties, I had gone only a few months without some intense emotional and physical connection to a member of the opposite sex: what in the desiccated, pseudo-therapeutic terminology of contemporary capitalism is called "a relationship." For the next five or six years, I had no long-standing romantic attachments. There were a few questionable and rather casual encounters that amounted to little. However, I formed several very close friendships with women, two of which were particularly important to me: those with Zulema and Rachel (both graduate students in the sociology program at UCLA).

There were three main reasons, in any case, for my state of quasi-isolation in LA. In the first place, I was fanatically determined to make a success of the opportunity offered by the university. In part this was because I finally felt like I was at a "real" institution: not a tenuous but interesting experiment like Eugene Lang College; very often I worked twelve- to fifteen-hour days and had no time or interest in much else. In my very early time at UCLA, I would get quite anxious if I had to spend more than about an hour doing something other than work. (This intensity subsided a bit later.)

The second factor to keep in mind is the socio-physical layout of LA. With no functional car (on my dad's advice, I had idiotically purchased a 1966 Lincoln that was wildly impractical), little money, and the status of a graduate student in sociology in a city of script writers and actors, my appeal as a potential mate hovered somewhere between a homeless person and a grocery store bagger. In other words, I was a loser.

The final factor had to do with my newfound capacity to distinguish between emotional and physical intimacy. Prior to LA, these two things had always gone together for me, but I discovered that emotional intimacy was possible with people with whom I was not physically intimate, and in fact it was in certain respects easier.

Zulema and Rachel were both quite brilliant, but a study in contrasts. The first, a second-generation daughter of Mexican immigrants from Fresno, was (and is) probably the toughest person I have ever known. Despite our different backgrounds, we shared certain character traits: we were both extremely ambitious, slightly pugnacious, prone to paranoid conspiracy theories, and a bit reckless. For these reasons we also both enjoyed crappy Hollywood horror movies. We also both shared a feeling of "imposter syndrome" at graduate school, where we met in the PhD program, although she could not see this since she interpreted "white privilege," with which in her eyes I was liberally endowed, as a kind of credit card that one carried around in one's wallet and presented at appropriate times and places.

Rachel was completely different; she was very fragile emotionally and would often express this by lashing out at her closest friends. Despite her substantial intellectual gifts, she also had a pathological lack of ambition, which I often, and perhaps wrongly, interpreted as a sign of "aristocratic" insouciance. I enjoyed talking to her immensely, but she also drove me crazy, and I was finally exhausted by her. Our friendship did not last beyond graduate school—or, to be more precise, beyond my marriage to Emanuela, who quite frankly could not stand her: a definite conflict of national character stood behind this.

Coda

Each of these losses before I met Emanuela was the destruction of a world; my early childhood before the divorce, my love for Amy, and my love for Stephanie were each complexes of internal emotional states and external ways of being. Thus, each loss was absolute and irrecuperable: the collapse of a totality. The contours between before and after are so sharp that I am almost tempted to refer to them as different lives, but in truth they cannot be so understood, since they are still lodged in *my* consciousness, and available for review. Was there a process of growth or learning? I hesitate between two impulses: one is to enchain the losses in a progressive narrative. The other is to reject this and to face each in itself. Somehow, one must live with irreconcilable ideas: each world's disappearance was tragic. But the losses themselves were also keys that opened doors—keys that I did not know I had until I used them. Without the divorce, would I have met Amy? It is unlikely, since presumably we would have moved to New Orleans, where maybe I would have come across a girl from Hammond—but probably not. I would also not have had that experience of being "a child of divorce" that was so much a part of what Amy and I shared, and that was one of the things that lent such great significance to what we had.

Without the loss of my first love, would I have met my second? Clearly not, since I would neither have been *where* I was, nor would I have been in the emotional state that allowed me to open and then walk through that door.

Without the infinitely sad disintegration of what Stephanie and I had, it is unlikely I would have gone to California; and without Amy's final refusal, I would not have been on Via Genova that day. The great difficulty is to recognize this while not falling into the temptation to allow the consequences to redeem the cause. The pain must be faced directly and without the anesthesia of its sequels.

I have traversed, so far in this volume, the foothills of my losses; what stands before me is a massive peak. I now must confront this one, which is as total and devastating as the love from which it emerged was unconditional and absolute. *Lasciate ogni speranza.*

Noi

Heat and Pain

Heat: oppressive, humid, laden with exhaust. Tramping down Rome's Via Nazionale, perhaps a bit overdressed. Turning to the left onto Via Genova, the noise and bustle quickly fade under the shadows of the lovely nineteenth-century buildings that loom over the street. A small button set inside a speaker; the flat buzz of the *citofono* (entry phone). "Sì?" (Yes?) "Sono uno studente americano." (I'm an American student.) That was the first conversation. It must have been the second week of September 1998. Emanuela told me quite firmly, with more than a hint of irritation, that the Fondazione Ugo Spirito opened at ten and that I was at least thirty minutes early.

Pain: she can no longer escape it. She needs me constantly to reposition her in the chair. I have to push her legs back into the recliner, lifting up one at a time. I can feel her body wasting away. She gives me a kiss on the top my head. These moments are so precious I try to lose myself in them. We are so close. She leans forward and whispers, "Ti amo così tanto; come faccio senza di te?" (I love you so much; what am I going to do without you?) I can only melt at the poignancy of the question. I think to myself, "Potrei farti la stessa domanda" (I could ask you the same question), but I don't say anything.

How did we get from there to here?

Citofono

It was Professor Alceo Riosa, I believe, who was entirely responsible for our meeting. Marco Santoro, with whom I had been in contact on the recommendation of Mabel Berezin, who was then teaching at UCLA, first connected me with the *professore*. Riosa and I had a couple of conversations about revolutionary syndicalism and the *sinistra fascista* (fascist left).* At least one of these took place in his office, a large space on the ground floor of the Università Statale di Milano with a number of desks, behind one of which sat one of his students, Barbara, who was pleasant and open but seemed old enough to be a full professor. Another of these unfolded in the little bar near the Statale, as the university is known, and which was also frequented by a group of aging *partigiani* (partisans) who would gather to drink beer and reminisce about killing Nazis and *repubblichini*.† Apparently I did not make a complete idiot of myself; I must have somehow managed to produce two or three coherent sentences about Sorel, and Riosa's skepticism softened somewhat. It helped also that I knew Perry Anderson, about whom we had a couple of conversations. "Devi andare a Roma" (You need to go to Rome), he said. "Cerca la Fondazione Ugo Spirito, e controlla l'Archivio Centrale dello Stato." (Look for the Fondazione Ugo Spirito and check out the Central State Archive [herafter ACS].)

I must have first come across Ugo Spirito's name in Emilio Gentile's book on fascist ideology.‡ The little I knew about him fascinated me. Spirito could best be described as a kind of left-wing dissident within the fascist regime. He claimed that the fascist revolution was incomplete in that it had not addressed

---

*   This expression may strike the reader as odd, but it was a feature of Italian fascism. The fascist left came from the tradition of Italian syndicalism, and its members were often followers of Georges Sorel.

†   This last expression refers to the supporters of the Nazi puppet regime called the *Repubblica di Salò* (Salò Republic), which ran the North of Italy from September 1943 to May 1945. The word *repubblichini* differs from *repubblicani*, which would indicate general support for a republican as opposed to a monarchical form of government. Both terms could be translated as "republicans," but they have a very different meaning.

‡   *Le origini dell'ideologia fascista (1918–1925)*, Rome, 1975. Translated as *The Origins of Fascist Ideology*, New York, 2005.

the question of private property; after a period of serving as a kind of intellectual ornament, he was eventually shunned for supposedly Bolshevik sympathies and spent the later years of the *ventennio* (the twenty-year period of fascist rule, 1922–42) in a kind of internal exile. In the postwar period he reemerged as a Maoist (this was in the fifties, well before this was a fashionable position). In any case, I purchased a train ticket to Rome and headed down.

After Emanuela had turned me away from the Fondazione, I passed the half hour with a *caffè e cornetto* (espresso and a crois-sant) at the bar directly under the place. Returning at ten o'clock, I was this time buzzed in. I passed through a large wooden door, the *portone* (external door), which opened into a courtyard. To the left was the entrance to an aging marble staircase that surrounded an old elevator shaft encased in black-painted steel mesh. The ele-vator itself was made of wood and had glass windows. It looked very much like an antique phone booth. Somewhat skeptical of its safety, and my ability to operate it, I elected to walk up. The Fondazione was on the third floor.

So many feet had trudged up the white marble stairs that each had a slight indent, to which I in some way contributed as my steps echoed up. On the third floor there was another *citofono*, and another buzz. "Sì?" (Yes?) "Sono lo studente." (I'm the student.) After much unbolting of locks the heavy gray door swung inward. There, standing in the corridor, was Emanuela's friend Francesca Garello, who regarded me with a mixture of skepticism and pity. She was tall, with a slightly horsey face and intelligent eyes. I tried to string together a few sentences explaining my project—something about intellectuals, fascism, and the *sinistra fascista*. I don't think I mentioned Sorel. She recommended that I consult the holdings on Giuseppe Bottai and ushered me in to the *sala studio* (reading room), which was later redesignated the *Sala Renzo De Felice* (The Renzo De Felice Room), after the historian of Italian fascism.[*] Bottai was one of the most peculiar and interesting figures of the period: a mix of conformism and ambition who sought to present fascism as a kind of third way between the decadent, liberal West and Stalinism. (Spirito's papers were not yet well archived, but Bottai's had been, and for various reasons those archival holdings were richer.)

I was the only person in the room. Its walls were painted a light blue; the floor was brown ceramic tile. There were a couple of rather new-looking tables with faux-wood veneer. A photograph of Ugo Spirito with his doughy features and placid eyes looked down at me. *La dottoressa* Garello brought me the catalogue.[†] I filled out some requests, which were whisked away. Then I waited. I could hear some bustling behind a set of double doors. They opened, revealing a room with a high bookshelf laden with archival boxes, towering above a crowded desk. I saw Emanuela working at the computer, a massive early nineties-era desktop. She was wearing a red-flannel shirt opened to reveal a blue tank-top; her pants were army green and rolled up above her purple Doc Marten boots, which matched her glasses. Her sparkling eyes were directed to the room where I sat. The effect was some kind of Italian version of Seattle grunge: which means, it was more stylish and colorful than the West Coast original.

Emanuela had a natural elegance about her; there was no hint of dolled-up fussiness. *This is me*, she seemed to be saying. *Who*

---

[*]   Perry Anderson's blistering analysis of De Felice in *Italia dopo l'Italia*, Rome, 2014, 96, is largely justified. However, De Felice's work remains fundamental to the study of the regime, especially the first three volumes of his massive biography of Mussolini.

[†]   Persons with a *laurea* (essentially the equivalent of a master's degree) are referred to as "doctor" in Italy.

the hell are you? She looked back at me; I'm not sure that we said anything. I was still a bit ashamed about our earlier interaction, and assumed that she must be slightly annoyed with "lo studente americano." I found her extremely attractive, but I gave it no more thought than that. The door closed, and I spent the morning, until *pausa pranzo* (lunch break), pouring over Bottai's somewhat tedious lectures on corporatism and requesting photocopies. Garello now disappeared and Emanuela began to bring me the documents I requested. I noticed this but made nothing of it. We exchanged a few words: "Grazie." "Prego." But I was completely absorbed in trying to figure out what was in front of me and was frankly paying little attention to much else.

I must have worked in the Fondazione for two or three days. The whole point of this first trip in 1998 was to identify potentially interesting troves of documents that I could exploit on a longer grant—hopefully a Fulbright. The atmosphere, which had initially been somewhat formal, began to warm. By the second day the doors to the offices and the archive had opened, I could hear laughter, and people were asking me what I wanted for lunch. After I had gotten a sense of the holdings at the Fondazione, my plan was to look for other materials at the ACS. At the end of the third day I said goodbye to the staff, and on the fourth I made my way to the archive.

The contrast between the Fondazione and the ACS was total: the first was located in a historic building in the center of Rome, the second in a huge modernist marble structure in the Esposizione Universale di Roma (Rome Universal Exposition, or EUR) suburbs to the south.* The entrance was on the ground

---

* EUR is a neighborhood built under the fascist regime for the World's Fair of 1942, which never took place. After the war it was used to house governmental buildings and apartments. The area has many emblematic fascist-modernist

floor and felt a bit like a bank; there was thick glass and a microphone. The attendant checked my passport and indicated that the catalogues and the reading room were on the second floor (*il primo piano*). I ascended the stairs, which opened out into a modern room with wooden floors and white plaster walls. I first had to speak with the archivist, who asked me some perfunctory questions about my project, after which she showed me the catalogues. I leafed through these, filled in my requests, and waited for the next document delivery, which took about an hour. (A lot of time "working in an archive" is spent sitting around waiting for boxes of material to arrive.)

When the boxes came, I entered the sala studio, a large attractive room finished in some sort of dark wood with long windows offering views of EUR and the surrounding countryside. I found the desk assigned to me (every *studioso* [scholar] has a number), and the boxes were delivered. I began to leaf through them. After about an hour of working, I turned around, and two or three rows behind me I saw her. Emanuela had come, I thought entirely by chance, to the ACS. She acknowledged me, and we both turned back to our boxes.

After a couple of hours of work, I decided to take a *pausa caffè* (coffee break). The ACS, like many Italian archives, was furnished with an automatic espresso vendor located in a kind of break room that was all white marble and glass. The choices were simple: caffè, cappuccino, caffè ristretto, caffè zuccherato. I deposited my 500 lire (about 50 cents at the time; this was before the introduction of the euro) and made my selection. The tiny plastic cup dropped down and the machine began to make a noise like a

---

buildings such as the *colosseo quadrato* (square colosseum) and the building that houses the archives itself.

power drill. In a few seconds espresso appeared. I turned around, and there she was. "Ciao," I said. "Su che cosa stai lavorando?" (What are you working on?)* She said something about working on her *tesi di laurea* (undergraduate thesis). We talked for several minutes about the collection and about the Fondazione Ugo Spirito. At that point I did something that seems a little reckless in hindsight. "Vorresti cenare con me stasera?" (Would you like to have dinner with me this evening?) It was one of the many times early in our relationship when a door seemed to appear that, if not walked through immediately, would close forever. To my astonishment, she replied, "Sì," and we made plans.

How we got to dinner is a bit unclear to me. Most likely Emanuela picked me up from my hotel, which was some wretched place near the train station, Termini, and took me on her *motorino* (scooter) to Trastevere, a bohemian neighborhood on the other side of the Tiber River from the ancient and modern city's central buildings (hence the name, which means "across the Tiber"), where the restaurant, La Fraschetta, was located.† We both ordered *bucatini all'amatriciana* and a beer. Somehow, we were able to communicate. We talked for at least two hours at the restaurant, and then she showed me around the *quartiere* (neighborhood).

After getting a frozen yogurt, we walked around and ended up at Piazza Sidney Sonnino, where we each smoked a cigarette.‡

---

* We were at this point on informal terms, as indicated by the conjugation of the verb *stare* to *stai* rather than *sta*.

† The word *fraschetta* literally means "twig"; it originally referred to a kind of temporary tavern where one could drink wine. The proprietor would hang a branch, usually of laurels, outside the door. Today the word is used in the region around Rome to refer to a relatively informal restaurant. But it is also often used as the proper name of a restaurant.

‡ Sidney Sonnino was a conservative liberal politician in the late nineteenth and early twentieth centuries famous for penning the article "Torniamo

Having run out of topics of conversation, I decided to raise the issue of Sonnino's historical significance. She laughed at me and said something to the effect of "È incredibile. Sto qui con un americano che mi sta parlando di Sidney Sonnino." (It's incredible. I'm here with an American who is talking to me about Sidney Sonnino.) Our evening ended. I took the train the next evening to Sicily to visit my sister-in-law and tour the Greek ruins at Agrigento, before returning to Milan.

What exactly had happened? It was a sort of date, but there seemed to be no realistic possibility of a romance. After all, the basic facts were these: I had come to Italy on a one-month training grant and had to return to Los Angeles, where I would apply for a Fulbright to go to Milan, not to Rome. Emanuela had an extremely busy life with two jobs and serious family responsibilities. It was pleasant to daydream about possibilities, but the likelihood that anything would happen between us seemed—because it was—infinitesimally small. Our connection was radically improbable, and that is key to who we were.

Probabilities

After I returned to LA, she sent me a letter with her photo. "I don't know if you remember me," it opened in English. "Now," it continued, "I write in my own language." Of course I remembered her; I remembered everything about her. I thought about her every day. She had also sent a photo of herself. She was slender, tan, attractive with intelligent, piercing eyes; it was from a trip to Greece that she had taken. It must have been 1996 or

---

allo Statuto" (Let's go back to the statue) published in 1897, which called for a strengthening of the monarchy and a weakening of parliament with the hopes of creating a structure like the German Empire.

1997. I remember her recounting it. The gas station attendant who made fun of her and her friends yelling "Mussolini" and thrusting out his jaw, her irritation at her friends' attraction to the beach when she wanted to see the culture and travel in the interior, something about a bee-sting and a visit to the hospital. It sounded like a bit of a nightmare. But the photo did its job; she was even more present to me than before. We began to correspond via email.

Our connection, then, depended on what was then still a very new technology; it would have been impossible even a few years earlier. I tried to explain my life, she hers. What did we understand of one another? Next to nothing, I suppose. Still, we formed a bond, sharing frustrations, explaining relationships. But the key piece of information I told her was that I was applying for a Fulbright to go back to Italy. She was immediately convinced that I would get it; I was much more skeptical and worried about when I would have to tell her I had been turned down and wouldn't be able to return.

I don't remember the day I received the news that I had been awarded the money, but I do remember telling her I was coming. I was standing in the kitchen in my father's house in Napa, California. It must have been in early summer or late spring. The midmorning light was pouring in the window above the kitchen sink. I heard the punctuated buzz of the Italian line as the phone rang there, then "Si, pronto." (Hello.) I have no idea what I said. There was rather a lot to communicate.

I had to tell her that I was coming, I had to tell her that I would be located in Milan, and I had to try to coordinate a meeting. Speaking on the phone is the most difficult thing to do in a foreign language because the speakers lack the visual cues that ease face-to-face communication. But somehow, I think I was able to convey the main points. I remember thinking that she seemed a bit disappointed by how complicated my situation was. On top of this, it turned out that my arrival dates coincided with her trip to New York, organized by the parents of her ex-boyfriend, Mario and Patrizia. (I found this a bit peculiar.) But somehow, we did establish a date to meet. Even in those early interactions, when we barely knew one another at all and were thousands of miles away, I could feel her warmth. Where was I going to stay? Had I found an apartment? And how was I going to navigate Milan, full, as it was, of *milanesi* (a human variety of whom she was always skeptical)?

I had applied to do a Fulbright in Milan on the basis of my master's paper research, which was focused broadly on the development of agrarian capitalism in Lombardy in the eighteenth century. (My first article was on this topic.) However, I had switched focus for the dissertation, which was initially conceived as a study of intellectuals in Italian fascism. My strategy was to show up in Italy and then tell the Fulbright committee that I had a new research subject. I figured it was unlikely they would kick me off the grant since it would be more trouble than it was worth. I was correct about that.

The Fulbright Commission showed virtually no interest in the content of my work, so long as I filled out their forms and could show that I was doing something. However, the changed research focus also raised other major problems. There are some interesting holdings in Milan for the interwar period, but any serious study of Italian fascism requires work at the ACS. This combined felicitously with the fact that Emanuela was there. But for the first few months of my time in Italy (I think I moved to Rome in February or early March), I was in Milan while she was in Rome.

How did all this work? When I first arrived in Milan, I had nowhere to live. (While I have always been very good about meeting academic deadlines, planning other aspects of my existence has never been a particular strong suit.) After several false starts, I fell into a great living situation in a large and comfortable apartment with interesting roommates on the Viale Papiniano. Four of us lived there: Giuliano, the official renter and the guy who organized the apartment; Stefano, a very friendly graphic designer who fancied himself much more worldly and sophisticated than he was; Kathrin, a Swiss student studying Italian art and architecture; and myself. As the two foreigners, Kathrin and I became particularly close. We would practice our Italian together, to the great amusement of Stefano and Giuliano. Sometimes we would use archaic words. I remember us talking about *il bidone della spazzatura* (an expression that few Italians would use, probably sounding something like "the receptacle for trash") and *mansuefare* (an old word for "tame," which one of us had come across somewhere), which sounded hilarious to the native speakers. My room was quite large, with white plaster walls, and a tall ceiling. The window looked directly out onto the *viale* (boulevard), and it had *tapparelle*, a kind of rolled-up shutter that could be pulled down by means of a flat cloth chord. I owned basically nothing: two sets of clothes, a computer (an old IBM laptop that still functions perfectly to this day), and one dried rose that I hung upside down on the wall. As time wore on, I collected books. My "bed" was a single mattress on the floor.

During this period, I took several trips to Rome; the first of these was crucial, but my memories here are blurred. One of the other Fulbright students in Milan was a woman named Christa. She was probably fifteen years older than me and was studying something about the history of Italian musical instruments. She asked if I wanted to take a trip with her to Scapoli, a town in Molise, in the South, where there was a "Museo della Zampogna"; a *zampogna* is a kind of bagpipe, versions of which are played throughout Italy. (Such instruments are played all over Europe, and they are very ancient, probably predating the Roman Empire.) I remember taking the trip down to Rome; this must have been in September of 1999 or so. Our idea was to rent a car there and then head south. Christa was very funny but had horrible Italian. She loved the expression *Mi da fastidio* because of the irritation, *fastidio*, being "given" to one by the offending object or person; I remember her anglicizing the expression, "*x* is really giving me fastidio" and us laughing about it. My Italian was a little better than hers, but, more importantly, I simply wasn't afraid to make errors and babble on until I managed to communicate something. I would make up words (*sperevolmente* for "hopefully," for example) and poke around until I'd managed to string together a sort of sentence.

I remember arriving at Termini, Rome's central train station, with Christa, getting off the train, and seeing Emanuela. We had arranged to meet. "Lovely" is too mild an expression. Christa later said she looked "delicious," which is better. She had on her purple crochet hat, which perfectly offset her hair and eyes. She was wearing an overcoat and gray pants. It all had the effect of perfectly framing her face and the little mole on the end of her nose. She had come, I think, directly from her office at the Tavola Valdese (a nonprofit organization where she worked at the time). I'm sure we embraced, although our official status was somewhat ambiguous. What I do remember is knowing that this was the woman I wanted to spend the rest of my life with. She was so warm, so beautiful, so completely perfect for me.

For some reason, we could spend only a limited time together. She may have been getting ready to leave for New York, and in any case I was supposed to drive Christa, who I think did not know how to drive a stick shift, to Molise. Later, Emanuela told me that she was very troubled by the whole idea of me traveling with Christa. *Chi cazzo è questa?* (Who the fuck is this girl?) she said she thought to herself. That, I thought, was pretty amusing given that Christa was almost old enough to be my mother.

Beginnings

When was the first kiss? I know where it was, although the exact date escapes me. We had a date at Fiesta y Siesta, a Mexican restaurant near Porta Pia, the spot where the Italian Bersaglieri had breached the defenses of Rome and completed the unification of the country in 1870. She loved the place because it had strawberry margaritas, which I think were her favorite drink at the time, and she was good friends with the owner, Luigi. I remember being amused by the menu, which was organized according to the Italian categories of *primo*, *secondo*, and *dolce*, but which had vaguely Mexican dishes. (These were really quite tasty, but they had only a distant relationship to the cuisine they ostensibly represented.)

We must have gotten quite drunk; God only knows what we talked about, as I could still barely speak Italian, and she was always overly cautious about English. As we were saying our goodbyes under the light of one of those buzzing and crackling orangish-yellow Roman streetlamps, I leaned toward her and kissed her: *un bacio appassionato* (an impassioned kiss), as she would have said. I think she may have been a bit taken aback, but not terribly so. I think if we had not kissed then, it's quite probable that we would have gone our separate ways. There are certain moments in life that must be seized, and if they are not, the opportunities they present never return; I have no doubt that that evening was one.

That kiss opened the door to an entirely different reality; from that point forward, our lives were totally bound up with one another, and they would not be unbound again until January 21, 2022. We were constantly traveling back and forth from Milan to Rome. She came several times to the apartment at Viale Papiniano. Milan was slightly foreign to her: the nasal accents, the cold brusqueness of the city's denizens. I remember her being overjoyed when the Milanese subway was running late. "Ecco. E dicono che le cose non funzionano a Roma!" (There you go. And they say nothing works in Rome!) But she liked to come to the apartment, and she set about trying to civilize me to some extent. "Com'è possibile che l'unica cosa che mangi è riso pronto?" (How is it possible that you only eat instant rice?) We went to the grocery store to buy actual food, and cooked together. We made love very often on my ridiculous little mattress. I have no idea how we didn't end up hurting ourselves or falling on the floor. But we didn't.

To some extent, we explored Milan; she liked the sandwiches at Bar Magenta, and we found a little Sicilian restaurant just across the street from the apartment called, appropriately enough, Il Padrino. The waitress had exactly one tooth, and they made a fantastic *pasta alla Norma*. There was a *locale* (a spot) nearby called Cuore (named after Edmondo De Amicis's novel) where we sometimes went, but it was so saturated with Milanese chic that we both found it a little tedious. I also remember one exquisite evening on the Navigli in Milan with my friend Marco Santoro and his partner at the time, Antonella. We also spent a lot of time in bookstores—either the ones selling used books on the Navigli, or the Feltrinelli (a popular bookstore) at Piazza del Duomo. But Emanuela usually preferred that we eat in; so often our outings were to the local "Spar" supermarket and occasionally to see a film.

Then there was Rome. I made several trips down before the final move. I loved the journey; the train basically follows the route of the ancient Roman Via Aemilia, running at angle toward the Southeast, along the southern edge of the Po Valley, until Bologna, where it drops due south over the Apennine Mountains to Florence. From there it wends its way through the Val d'Orcia in southern Tuscany toward Lazio and then to the eternal city. The countryside changes dramatically during the journey: from the gray, low-hanging sky and fertile agriculture lands of the Po watershed to the jagged peaks of the Apennines, and then emerging into the dry yellow hills of Tuscany. The overall impression is a movement from cold to warm, from gray to golden, from dark to light. (It is no accident that the South in Italy is called the *Mezzogiorno*, "midday," the place where the sun resides.) Of course, for me, the fact that Emanuela lived in Rome intensified all these sensations immensely.

Where did I stay during those early trips? Emanuela was living, temporarily, at her friend Francesca's house (the one who had opened the door for me at the Fondazione Spirito) but had started to look for an apartment for us. The plan was that as soon as she found one, we would move in together. Looking back, it's hard to believe our recklessness. We had barely met, and yet were making one of the most consequential decisions a couple can. In any case, in those first few months in Italy, I would often stay at my friend Ian's, whom I had met on the initial Fulbright retreat to Amalfi. He was an enthusiastic "critical realist" who had become quite disillusioned with his rather tedious-sounding art history project, and who was envious of the German Fulbright group. I was immediately drawn to his sardonic humor, and we got on very well.

He used to fantasize about meeting a German *Mädchen* (maiden) on an upcoming trip, on which we were all invited, to Berlin, and he would prance around his large apartment off Piazza Cavour saying, "Entschuldigen Sie (Excuse me), young lady" in an affected southern accent to practice charming the *Berlinerinnen* (Berlin women); I don't think it worked at all.

I remember taking Emanuela to a dinner at his house with the other Fulbright students. She was a little nervous at being plunged into this world of strange *americani* (Americans). We arrived together on her motorino; I'm not sure where we had been before. She was glowing, her dark eyes flashing, her purple scarf and maroon leather jacket making her look like some elegant pilot from the 1920s. The dinner was Korean food prepared by Aliza Wong (now the director of the American Academy in Rome), who had helped me get my first apartment in Milan. It was a wonderful evening; I remember seeing Emanuela's face relax as it wore on, and she found herself enjoying this strange collection of people.

The turn of the millennium fell at the very beginning of our romance. We passed it in Rome at an apartment not far from the Piazzale Flaminia, just off the Piazza del Popolo. The place was spacious but very "upholstered." The overall impression was deep red with soft golden light. In one room, the TV was broadcasting the latest scandal involving *Il Cavaliere* (literally "the knight," Berlusconi). Adjacent to it, through a set of French doors, was the dining room. It had a large oblong table covered with a white tablecloth, over which hung a chandelier. In the center of the table there was a bowl of pasta (rigatoni, I believe) *al tonno* (with tuna). It was not the usual red sauce in which I had seen this dish prepared before; it must have featured a lot of capers. "Dylan, proviamola." (Dylan, let's try it.) She got one bowl for the two of us to share. This was always her way in such situations; it signaled for her, I think, our absolute togetherness. I tried some of the pasta, which I found to be a bit stodgy. "Com'è?" (How is it?) she asked. "Buono" (Good), I lied.

She then issued a definitive judgment. "Per me è un po' pesante." (For me it is a little heavy.) Coming from Emanuela, this somewhat innocuous-sounding phrase was a devastating barb indicating utter culinary failure. A good dish was never "heavy." Our son, Eamon, would later learn how to use this judgment to his advantage. If he didn't like something, he would turn to Manu (as I would come to call Emanuela) and say, "Mamma, è un po' pesante." (Mom, it's a little heavy.) She laughed, "È proprio un paraculo"—an untranslatable expression roughly indicating someone adept at manipulating others, thus an "ass-coverer." We set the bowl of pasta aside.

Prosecco appeared; at midnight, we toasted the millennium and kissed; at that moment, we were still a very new item. But it already felt as if we would always be together. After the toasts, the guests, which included Emanuela's dear friend Gianni and his partner, Susanna, moved up to the roof, from which we watched the fireworks exploding over the Piazza del Popolo. At some point we left the apartment and formed part of the river of people that flowed toward the piazza itself. There was a strange excitement in the air, as if this particular *capodanno* (New Year) would usher in the apocalypse, a computer crash on a worldwide scale, or the return of the Messiah. For us, 2000 had a more intimate significance: it was a *spartiacque* (watershed). I was twenty-nine and she was thirty. The two of us stood on that threshold between "true adulthood" and whatever it is that comes before. We had found each other exactly at that point where decisions come to have a certain weight, where one's bets really begin to matter, as it were, and we had already gone all in for one another.

The evening ended with us taking Suzanna back to her house in Gianni's car. I learned, somewhat to my surprise, that Suzanna still lived with her parents; she must have been in her mid-thirties at the time; but that, as I came to understand, was entirely normal among Romans of her generation. This cast new light on a conversation Emanuela and I had had previously. We had been having a caffè at Termini. I think I must have been waiting for a train to return to Milan. She looked at me very seriously with her chocolate eyes. "Ti devo dire una cosa" (I need to tell you something), she said. I wasn't sure what to expect. Was it a husband, or a kid, that she hadn't told me about? "Mia sorella è molto malata e sono stata costretta ad uscire di casa a diciotto anni." (My sister is very sick, and I had to leave home at eighteen.) I was, of course, concerned about Simona's illness; Emanuela explained to me that her sister was schizophrenic, and that consequently she felt physically unsafe living in the same house with her. Indeed, at one point Simona had even thrown a pot of boiling water on Emanuela's leg; she later showed me the scar.

The one thing I did not quite understand, however, was the particular emphasis that Manu placed on her age; it seemed completely normal to me to leave home at eighteen. It was only at that New Year's evening that I really understood its significance. For her, leaving home at that age was a major violation of expectations for women—and, for that matter, also men of middle-class origins. The general family strategy is to stay at home and accumulate resources so that love, marriage, homeownership, and moving out from one's parents' house tend to closely coincide. In a way, the forced breaking apart of these phases had "Americanized" her before she ever met me, and must have been one of the factors that explained her totally uncharacteristic (for her class and culture) acceptance of my relative penury. This is not to say that she wasn't a bit taken aback at times by my precarious finances; "Ho trovato un americano pieno di debiti" (I found an American who is deep in debt), she would laugh. But somehow she trusted that I would figure things out, that my basic optimism would be self-fulfilling.

The move to the apartment on Via Scarpellini, in the Parioli district, is very clear in my mind. The apartment was a tiny one-room place with a "kitchen" in the doorway on the ground floor. It was in one of those cream-colored buildings put up in the thirties that is all curves and plaster, reflecting the city's extraordinary light. The *portiere* (doorman) had a little plastic sign that he would place on his desk that read "torno subito" (I'll be back soon), a statement belied by the hours it sat there. She met me at Termini and we got a taxi: a white Fiat "Panda" van, which resembled a slightly melted cube of ice cream. I had arrived in the early afternoon. We unpacked the bags, had a caffè, and spent most of the rest of the day trying out the futon, which was much more comfortable than my mattress in Milan.

We settled into a routine; she worked a lot, going first to her job at the Tavola Valdese, then to the Fondazione Ugo Spirito. In the mornings she would take me to the bus stop on her motorino and I would make my way out to the ACS, where I would spend the day poring over documents and trying to make photocopies. Occasionally we would meet for lunch or coffee near the Fondazione and then go home together. Archival work is lonely and anxiety provoking. I would constantly try new ideas out on her; she was encouraging, although sometimes skeptical. "Come fai a dimostrarlo con i documenti?" (How are you going to show that with the documents?) she would ask, a question to which I usually didn't have a great response. She would share her frustrations at work; she had a visceral hatred for any sign of laziness, incompetence, or corruption. Emanuela described herself as a *legalitaria*—a term indicating a kind of moral reaction to the laxity and corruption that is a fact of life in Italy. In her case it went beyond an observance of the law, to a broader insistence on doing things well; corners should not be cut; rules should in general be followed (except obviously unnecessary ones, like stopping at a stop sign when there were no cars in sight). Sometimes this frustrated me; but I grew to appreciate her insistence that life be lived with care.

We were having lunch at Brek, a sort of cafeteria restaurant at Largo Argentina (a Roman temple complex in a busy central location). I couldn't keep my eyes off her. She had on her office clothes, brown pants, and, I think, a gray sweater with a very fetching wool hat. This was her *donna manager* (career woman) outfit, as she called it. She moved to get up, but I told her it would be better to wait a bit as otherwise I would be embarrassed. She sat down with a mischievous twinkle in her eye, and asked if I wanted coffee. I said yes and we passed another fifteen or so minutes there before exiting.

Emanuela was a big enthusiast for video games, especially complex ones. She loved online fantasy (*Civilization* and *Zelda*, for example), and she took it all very seriously; our first fight broke out over my failure to save our progress in *Tomb Raider* (which she pronounced "Tome Rider"). I had somehow lost an entire level of progress, and she was so disgusted with me about it that she refused to speak for several hours.

Occasionally she would arrange to meet people from her online role-playing games in real life. For example, we met a couple of guys at a McDonald's in Milan, where they talked about elves and dragons over an order of chicken nuggets; at one point, back in Rome, she was invited to dinner at the home of a guy named Michele, who was also somehow connected to this world. We had to travel all the way to the end of the subway line; the neighborhood was an arid jumble of buildings, with unfinished cinder block and red-brick exteriors thrown up in haste without the slightest concession to urban planning. Michele was a few years older than us and had a relatively well-paying job that had allowed him to purchase one of these places. The interior, as is often the case in such neighborhoods, formed a complete contrast to the outside. It was spotlessly clean, with new furniture and a perfectly appointed table.

Michele gave us the obligatory house tour, which in Italy always starts in the bathroom. We admired the tiles, looked at his bedroom, and returned to the dining room to eat some dinner and chat, mostly about America: an easy and ready topic of conversation built into my identity, as it were. (I imagined myself as a life-sized doll with a label reading "Boyfriend: Ready Topics of Conversation Included.") But his eyes were sad, and I could see his longing as he looked at her. Was she oblivious to the fact that Michele had planned this as a date for the two of them? Or had she brought me along precisely because she *was* aware? I raised the topic on the way back: "È chiaro che Michele è innamorato di te" (It's clear that he's in love with you). "Non essere ridicolo," she replied. "È solo un amico." (Don't be ridiculous; he is only a friend.) There was nothing more to say. Emanuela's definitions of reality, in any case, had a strong tendency to self-realization.

For some reason we had to sit the family dog, "Drugo" (the Italian name for "the Dude" in *The Big Lebowski*), a couple of times. He was a black Chihuahua with the head of a much-larger animal, perhaps a German shepherd, stuck on his tiny body that bore no physical resemblance to his namesake, and whose nervous and agitated character was the antithesis of California cool. Our first experience was at Sandra and Matteo's place on Via Riccardo Foster. The idea was to pass a pleasant evening together at her parents' spacious apartment; the dog, however, had other plans. At the slightest sign of amorous contact, he would bark hysterically until we stopped. We had to sneak around the house like two sheepish teenagers under the watchful eye of some deranged, overprotective uncle (or was it a jealous lover?) until he finally went to sleep.

The second time we watched him, he stayed at our one-room apartment on Via Scarpellini, where there was a strict no-pet policy. My strategy was to exercise Drugo sufficiently that he would sleep most of the time, and hopefully not bark. I took him on long runs around Villa Gloria and tried to train him to follow the lead by deploying a technique my eldest brother, Evan, had taught me back in Louisville. If I saw an obstacle, such as a pole, I would pass by it closely. If Drugo was not paying attention to where I was, his collar would be pulled sharply. By the end of the second day of running this way, the dog was completely focused on me, realizing that this was the best way to avoid a nasty jerk.

After these runs he was completely exhausted, and thus slept soundly and quietly most of the day. I think Emanuela found my techniques a bit too strict; like her dad, Matteo, she indulged all animals. When we would come back after one of the training sessions, she would say, "Poverino, è stanco da morire" (The poor little guy is dead tired), as he flopped down and lapped water from his bowl.

Some months after we had moved into the apartment, she was sitting on the futon wearing a slightly improbable pink sweat-suit. It was a weekend morning and we had just had our caffè and cornetto. Her eyes were smiling and relaxed as the light streamed in. "Ci sposiamo?" (Should we get married?), I asked in an absurdly offhand way. "Sì," she said. Then we kissed and visited the Mercato Traiano.

She remembered this same event slightly differently. For her, it went like this. We were wandering around the Mercato looking in on ancient shops where merchants had sold olive oil, wine, and perhaps wheat in amphorae. In one of the rooms, a large trove of these was stacked in the corner, so that one could almost imagine being in a fully stocked *bottega* (store) sometime in the early second century. "Ci sposiamo?" I said. To which she replied, "Sì!" In either case, this momentous decision, like most of the others that we made together, was rapid and almost casual.

After we decided to marry, several things had to be done. One was to tell Emanuela's father about the decision. Matteo and I were sitting in two red upholstered chairs at the apartment on Via Riccardo Foster. We were angled toward one another, but not directly facing, lending a slightly abstract feeling to the conversation. It must have been a Sunday, when we would have *il pranzo della domenica* (Sunday lunch) with them; we had probably also had a *cassata siciliana* (best described as a cannolo in the form of a cake) from Pasticceria Dagnino for dessert, and had surely moved on to grappa; my senses were fogged and I felt warm and comfortable. It seemed the moment to *affrontare l'argomento*—to confront the issue. I said something to the effect of "Abbiamo deciso di sposarci." (We've decided to marry.)

Emanuela was in the kitchen or in her room, or perhaps on the *terrazzo* (balcony) that overlooks *i Castelli Romani* (the mountains just outside of Rome). I could sense the resistance from the other chair. "Sai, Dylan, in Sicilia c'è un detto: moglie e buoi dei paesi tuoi." (You know, Dylan, in Sicily there is a saying: oxen and wives from one's own village.) I replied with something about love and multiculturalism, like I was reciting language from the brochure of the Fulbright Commission.

It was a strange and difficult exchange; it felt as if we were both playing roles that weren't really us at all. To me, Matteo's objection seemed almost pro forma and oddly impersonal; it was something that he felt he had to say, a *dovere del padre* (a father's duty). He probably felt, in particular, that his mother—with whom he was very close, even if it was a difficult closeness—wanted him to say it. It was the first and last time that Matteo ever expressed reservations about our marriage. Once it became obvious that the decision was final, he quickly resigned himself to the facts and became once again practical and warm.

We also had to tell Nonna Angiola; she was a dignified, elegant, and strong woman living alone in a beautiful flat in Via Savoia near Piazza Fiume. In the stairwell of her building was a plaque commemorating several victims of *Nazifascismo* (a combined term referring to both main Axis powers) who had lived there before the war. Like the Fondazione Spirito, it had a telephone booth elevator, but this one, unlike the exemplar on Via Genova, was well maintained, with its brass gleaming, its windows clean, and its wood shining.

Her apartment had high ceilings and wooden floors; its rooms were arranged along a corridor. Upon entry there was a little room to the right covered with eighteenth- and nineteenth-century prints where she would watch television. To the left, just down the corridor, was the entrance to the *soggiorno*, a spacious living room where on the weekends she would play canasta with her friends from the building. On the wall opposite the corridor was a set of French doors that opened onto the terrazzo that overlooked Via Savoia and was laden with plants.

The most striking thing about the room was the built-in bird-cage framed by ceramic tiles, representing plants and flowers, that was located between the terrazzo and the soggiorno. Its outside wall was a window, and the inside was a set of bars. The bird, presumably, could enjoy the illusion of being out of doors this way; when we were there, however, it had been converted into a greenhouse and was full of houseplants.

Emanuela was very close to Nonna Angiola; they had even lived together for a while before the jealousy of *le ʒie* (the aunts) somehow intervened to put a stop to this. I could sense the fierce pride that her grandmother felt for Emanuela—the first in the family to get a laurea and the one who could always be relied upon to solve family difficulties or arrange things.

Christmas of 2000 brought home to me her centrality to the family. Everyone was there in the apartment on Via Savoia. Cecilia had been explaining to Tommaso that all of the dead relatives were looking down at him from their places in *cielo* (heaven), to which Tommaso responded, "E perché stanno tutti a guardare me?" (And why are they all looking at me?) Manu had on her red sweater, a white shirt, and black pants that made her dark eyes and striking face stand out all the more. She was organizing the distribution of the presents. I noted how everyone immediately deferred to her. "Che cosa dice Emanuela?" (What does Emanuela say?) She decided the order of the distribution of the presents and seemed to understand exactly what they all were. Nonna Angiola asked her how people should be arranged around the dinner table where we ate *lasagna con carciofi* (lasagna with artichokes). I remember thinking to myself, *What will they do if she moves to the US with me?* The family seemed to orbit around her, as our little unit would later do.

We brought some things from the pasticceria at the end of the block and had caffè. At some point, Emanuela told Nonna Angiola that we were going to marry. She took the news in stride, as I recall, not seeming particularly surprised. As we said goodbye, she grabbed my cheeks and looked into my eyes. "Falla felice!" (Make her happy!) she said. There was a lot in those words; she was saying appreciate her, support her, don't betray her, and above all love her without reservation. I tried; God knows I tried.

I am not entirely clear about exactly when or how we got from Via Scarpellini to the apartment in Monteverde. It must have gone something like this. I had to return to the US for a couple of months, in early summer 2000. We found together a new apartment in the neighborhood of Monteverde, but Emanuela had to do the physical move herself. It was near the Porta San Pancrazio and the Villa Doria Pamphili, a large park built on a seventeenth-century estate. The neighborhood was much livelier and more interesting than Parioli. Our building was on the Via Ludovico di Monreale at the piazza Ottavilla. Almost directly across from it was a pizzeria, and there was a *bar* (café) on the corner of the piazza and the Via Fonteiana. While we were living there, a *rosticceria* (lunch place) opened on the corner diagonally opposite the bar and basically directly under our house; it had excellent roasted chicken, potatoes, and *pomodori ripieni* (stuffed tomatoes). Often, when we were too tired to cook, we got takeout there. There was also a little *fruttivendolo* (fruit vendor) just off the piazza on the Via Ottavilla. The proprietor always called Emanuela *tesoro* (dear) and sold us tomatoes that were either delicious or slightly rotten, depending on the day and time.

Just down the Via Fonteiana there was a place that sold *mozzarella di bufala* (buffalo mozzarella); it was a retail outlet for a *cooperativa agricola* (agricultural cooperative) from the countryside around Lazio. Occasionally Emanuela would get one of the white creamy balls, and some ricotta, and we would eat it with a little salt, oil, and bread.

Our place was perched above the official top floor of the building, which must have dated from the twenties or thirties and was painted a light salmon color with cream trim that turned golden when the sun set. The apartment was clearly *abusivo* (not up to code); it was one of those precarious add-ons, carved out of preexisting storage spaces or cannibalized common areas, that are characteristic of many Italian buildings.

We had to pay the proprietors, a rather shady couple somehow connected to the Chiesa Valdese (the Waldensian Church that ran the non-profit where Emanuela worked), and whom I liked very little, in cash.* The place was tiny but very comfortable. What made it magical was the terrazzo, which was paved with terracotta tiles, had a white plastic table, an awning for protecting us from the brutal Roman summer sun, and a sink with a hose attached, with which we watered the plants and sometimes even showered.

From there, one could see across the whole neighborhood, all the multicolored awnings and little lawn chairs and the buildings brightly colored and stacked on top of one another like a child's building blocks. Saturday and Sunday mornings, we would hear the *arrotino* (knife sharpener), who would circulate through the neighborhood with a loudspeaker saying, "Venite, donne, donne belle, è arrivato l'arrotino, arruota coltelli, forbici,

---

* The Waldensians are a proto-Protestant branch of Christianity that broke with Catholicism in the early thirteenth century.

forbicine." (Come, women, beautiful women, the knife sharpener has arrived, he sharpens knives, scissors, clippers.)

The most peculiar feature of the place was the bathroom, a tiny space accessible through a miniature twisting staircase, and in which we could barely stand up. Taking a shower or bath in there required the skill of a master gymnast.

Our bed, a brownish-red fold-out couch, was a very slight upgrade from the futon at Via Scarpellini, but at the time it seemed like heaven to both of us. In the summer the place got very hot. We would sleep with the glass doors to the terrazzo open, but the outside screen door locked; *c'erano i ladri* (there were thieves).

One of our first disagreements was over the use of a tiny yellow fan that looked like it must have dated from the fifties. I wanted to leave it on all night, pointed directly at my head; Emanuela objected to this practice on two grounds. First, she never trusted that the thing wouldn't short out and cause a fire, and second, she was convinced that so much direct air over an entire night would somehow provoke illness. I had to concede the cogency of her first point; the thing really was an antique. But the second seemed completely unreasonable to me, based on fantastic folkloric notions that had no grounding. We compromised. I got to keep the fan on for the first hour every night.

This was where we were living when we had our first visitors as a couple. My brothers came: first Scott (Jessica's son, a year older than me), then Evan with Lida and Eva (my sister-in-law and niece). Scott stayed with us for a couple of weeks. It was a joy to show him around Rome; I even dragooned him into coming to the archives with me one day to help out with photocopying. There was a daily limit to the number of photocopies for each *studioso*—around fifty per person. By bringing Scott along,

I could double that quota. The photocopy guy, with whom I was on very good terms at that point, admired my plan. "Gli americani," he said, "sono sempre così pratici." (Americans are always so practical.)

When Evan, Lida, and Eva came to visit, they were on their way to Alcamo (a small town on the northern coast of Sicily, west of Palermo); I remember their arrival at the apartment because Emanuela spent most of the day preparing pomodori ripieni, and I was tasked with making sure the family got from Gianicolo to the apartment exactly on time. The following day, it may have been, we all went to the pride parade around the Circo Massimo, and Eva got an enormous gelato. By the time were back at our place, she was covered head to toe in sticky ice cream, and we showered her off directly on the terrazzo.

I remember one afternoon at that apartment—or perhaps it was many afternoons. I was washing the dishes, and Emanuela was *passando lo straccio per terra* (mopping the floor). She had on her brown cotton dress, and her hair was tied back in a red bandana. I turned to look at her and felt an overwhelming rush of desire. "Che stai facendo? Dobbiamo pulire casa!" (What are you doing? We need to clean the house!) she exclaimed. We took a long break and returned to finish up our cleaning in the late afternoon.

On the weekday summer mornings, I would often wake around five or six and make a caffè for both of us while she prepared to go to work; after she was gone, I would write on the terrazzo until around noon, when the sun became too strong. I would then go for a run in the Villa Pamphili and spend the rest of the day reading, cleaning the house, or shopping until she returned.

I loved being able to take care of her, to make her day a little better. I learned how to make a decent amatriciana, and pasta al tonno; but she often wanted something lighter: *un'insalata mista con pane* (mixed salad with bread), or sometimes *salumi e sottaceti* (cold cuts and pickles). Sometimes we would go to the market together with our little plaid *carrello* (cart) that she had purchased with the *punti* Spar (Spar points) that we collected from shopping. Her friends from university made fun of us for being *due vecchietti* (an elderly couple), but we didn't care; *faceva comodo quel carrello* (that shopping cart was convenient).

Those months, which are intense enough in memories to seem like years, were as close as I have ever come to paradise. We were young and completely in love, and finally had a place that really felt like ours. I would give anything in the world to have just one of the days at Via Ludovico di Monreale back.

Svizzera (Switzerland)

If anyone doubted the fundamental significance of national character, the train ride from Milan to Zurich would be enough to set them right. It was a business trip for Emanuela; I think she was going to check on the workings of a Swiss foundation that was funding a program to help Romanian street children; these were victims of the closure of Soviet-era orphanages and now condemned to live in tunnels under the streets of Bucharest. The plan was to stay with her colleague Inge and her partner, and also to visit Kathrin, my roommate from Milan who had returned home for Christmas.

After a brief trip through the hills near Lake Como, the train crosses the border at Chiasso. The station overlooks the town, which from that angle appears as a brightly colored jumble of tiles traversed by a tangle of traffic-engorged roads: a seething chaos. Life, in short. Emanuela peered out, exclaiming, "Guarda che casino!" (Look at the mess!) There was a hint in her voice of that particularly Italian tendency to loathe one's compatriots that, paradoxically, is one of the things that makes Italians so immediately identifiable as a national group.

After the passport check was complete, the train lurched forward and a curtain of order descended on the landscape: uniform houses, well-planned streets, spotless sidewalks. I thought to myself that I rather preferred the Italian side. At the stop after Chiasso, there was bustle and confusion as the army recruits stashed their M16s in the overhead baggage compartment above our heads and stuffed their backpacks with the distinctive Swiss Army cross into the spaces between the seats. We wended our way through Ticino, the Italian-speaking region of southern Switzerland, looking out at the absurdly picturesque countryside with its little white farmhouses and churches and contented-looking dairy cows, set off like the props of a child's train against the snow and bits of grass.

The Alps grew taller, and the language changed from Italian to German as we approached Zurich. Emanuela was wearing her checkered purple hat for that trip and was looking out curiously, as was I. When we arrived at the station, we noted the location of the "Meeting Point" for the purposes of connecting with Kathrin the following day. The idea of such a thing was not so ubiquitous at the time as it was later to become, and we interpreted it as a Swiss foible. We made our way to the tram stop, which was directly opposite the train station. There we were faced with an enormous printed schedule of baroque complexity. Emanuela looked at it skeptically. "Ci vogliono tre lauree per capire sta cosa!" (One needs three degrees to understand this thing!) After studying it for a bit, we found our tram's time. Needless to say, it was punctual and spotlessly clean. It took us to a little collection of low-lying houses overlooking the town. At the stop, we met Inge, who accompanied us back to her place; I believe it was on foot, although she may have had a car. She must have been in her early sixties, projecting an air of friendly seriousness. At the house, we met her partner, whom Emanuela referred to her as *la donna di Inge* (Inge's woman)—an athletic-looking blonde woman in her late thirties or early forties. We dined with them; they served us a very sensible fish dish with a healthy side of rice.

After dinner, we helped with the washing-up, which introduced us to what we interpreted, perhaps wrongly, as another Swiss peculiarity. La donna di Inge carefully washed each dish and set it into the drying rack immediately, without rinsing it; Emanuela and I exchanged glances but said nothing as the suds slowly slid off the plates; this was obviously how things were done. Was it water conservation? We never quite figured it out.

After the washing-up was done, we moved to the living room to plan the morning. Inge began the proceedings by asking us how long it would take to shower. Each of us gave a slightly different estimate: nine minutes, twelve minutes, fifteen minutes. Inge compiled the times and undertook some calculations. She then gave us the order of our showers and, after taking account of the seven minutes it would take to walk to the tram, told us what time we would need to wake, present ourselves for breakfast, and leave the house. After we retired to our room, Emanuela and I had a good laugh at the comical way that Inge was fulfilling the national stereotype. Naturally, the next morning, everything went off without a hitch.

Why do I have this memory? During that trip, she purchased, or we purchased together, or I purchased for her, a shoulder bag called a "Freitag." (Kathrin had told us that there were knock-offs of the original brand sold at grocery stores, under the name

"Donnerstag.") It's hanging now in the closet in my hallway. Made of recycled tarpaulin and old seatbelts, it will probably last until the end of the century. Like so many things that surround me, it bears stories. I must extract them before they are lost forever—which is, after all, my only hope of making Emanuela come alive in some way again. Among other things, I've become a miner of memories.

Carrozza

The Eurostar, the sleek, modern train with patriotic colors splashed across its low, bullet-like profile, was either late or had been canceled. But the other was available: *il locale* (the local). Its carriages were taller and less aerodynamic than the new train; they were softened rectangular solids linked together like so many slightly melted sticks of butter. The steps were also steeper and thus harder to negotiate with our bags. Instead of an open passenger cabin with seats off a central aisle, here there was a narrow passageway on one side of the car with doored compartments opening onto it.

We found a place and arranged our things. Emanuela and I at this point had been together long enough that she had been able to thoroughly Italianize my wardrobe, and she herself was always very stylish. I think she had her orange Mandarina Duck bag. Five or ten minutes after we had taken our seats, our traveling companion appeared: an elderly man wearing a blue gilet with gray pants and a blazer. He had brought with him a carefully packed lunch as well: altogether *un signore* (a gentleman), well dressed, carefully groomed, and polite. At some point Emanuela turned to me and said, "Guarda le sue unghie." (Look at his fingernails.) I looked at his hands and noticed his clipped and perfectly clean nails. He was probably about the same age as my grandfather, whose nails by contrast were always a bit yellow and overgrown, a situation that had worsened since my grandmother's passing. "Qualcuno," said Emanuela, "si cura bene di lui." (Someone takes good care of him.)

He was, she was saying, a loved person; and that fact seemed to elevate him in her eyes—perhaps because she thought that if someone cared so much for him, it must be a sign that he was the kind of person who merited it. I'm not sure that I quite understood what she saw in him and his well-manicured hands—or, if I did understand it, that I quite agreed with it. But what I did know is that I would care for her as much as I was able, and I was sure that she would do the same for me.

Land of the Free

We returned to the US the summer before our wedding. My grandfather (Hugh, whom Emanuela always called Ugo) was still alive, and the whole family greeted us at the airport. They had driven down in his enormous gray Lincoln that maneuvered like an aircraft carrier and made us all slightly queasy. Emanuela was in a state of profound culture shock. It was her first contact with California, her only prior experience of America having been Manhattan two summers before, which of course hardly counts.

She clutched her handbag, full as it always was of every imaginable useful item, and even of a few that were of questionable use, and refused to put it in the trunk. Her eyes were wide as she took in the enormous highway that snakes north from the San Francisco Airport, with its river of vehicles of every size and description. I truly realized only then how brave she was, how much she risked to bet on us, to bet on me; and I fell in love with her again. No one before Emanuela had ever placed this much trust in me, and never before Emanuela had I known what it felt to be with someone who believed in the absolute value of our togetherness. This trust was mutual; I had told her before we left Rome on the trip to the US that if she wanted to stay in Italy, I would find some way to make a career there. "Non essere ridicolo" (Don't be ridiculous), she said. I don't know if she ever realized that I was totally serious. This unreserved commitment to one another was one of the most precious things we had.

The plan was to take a trip through the American Southwest. We visited some of the major national parks: Bryce, Zion, and Mesa Verde, ending up at the family time-share, which is hardly ever used, in Angel Fire, New Mexico. My father had arranged a kind of reunion at this place: there was my aunt Julia and her husband, Garry; there was Uncle Bill and his wife, Mary Ellen; and then my grandfather, with his new girlfriend, Pauline—the founder of a chain of auto-parts stores from Texas and a rock-ribbed Republican of whom we were all quite skeptical. My brother Scott arrived later.

Garry insisted on talking to Emanuela about Italian sports cars; it would be hard to imagine a topic about which she was less interested and less informed. The only thing I remember about their exchange was her correcting his pronunciation of "Modena," which he called "Mod-EE-na." But she liked his affability and enthusiasm. One evening Emanuela decided to make bucatini all'amatriciana for everyone. But the family committed a fundamental faux pas. Just as the pasta was being drained, they all decided to exit the house for some walk or other. "Che cazzo stanno facendo?" (What the fuck are they doing?) she exclaimed. "La pasta è pronta!" (The pasta is ready!) I managed to herd them back to the table, where we enjoyed an excellent Roman meal in the middle of nowhere.

There is no better way, in any case, to experience the immensity of the US than that sort of tour. I felt very protective of Emanuela. One scene stands out. She was wearing her brown dress with a little white cotton sweater that covered her shoulders. We were somewhere in Utah, and she was making a call to her parents from a pay phone (they were not yet totally obsolete). She seemed fragile somehow. There, in the desert, so far from home. I felt a deep responsibility to ensure that no one in this strange land would harm her; as irrational as it may sound, with what happened later, I feel that I somehow failed in this most fundamental obligation, and that failure will haunt me forever.

The food on that trip was utterly mysterious to her—especially breakfast. One morning we were in Arizona. The desert heat, dry and intense, poured down from the sky and seeped out of the ground as in some enormous oven. She wanted *una colazione semplice* (a simple breakfast)—something recognizable, not vast and calorific. So she chose French toast, which she imagined must resemble *pane tostato* (toasted bread). When the enormous slabs arrived slathered with butter and swimming in fake maple syrup, she could only laugh. "Sti americani!" (These Americans!)

Emanuela was also fascinated and somewhat annoyed by the ubiquity of ice in American restaurants. In Utah, she asked for a glass of water without it—a request that prompted questions about where she was from. "Oh, my boyfriend went to Europe one time," the waitress declared. Did the word refer to a country, a continent, or just some undefined location filled with people who had unusual customs? It was unclear. What a strange place she had landed in, with all its rituals of waste and excess, so totally contrary to her own careful modesty about consumption.

At Zion, we hiked a steep trail that climbs up from the valley floor. It is punctuated by a series of natural pools formed in the rock. As we approached the largest one, we heard "O, senti che puzza di piedi!" (Ew, it smells like feet!) Emanuela was horrified. Here in the wilds of Utah, we had bumped into a large and garrulous group of not just Italians, but Romans. She absolutely forbade me to speak to her in Italian as we skirted by the group and made our way further up the valley floor.

I can still see her where we parked the car at Bryce. She had seen a chipmunk, and it was as exciting to her as if she had just glimpsed a wildebeest or an elephant in the wild. There were several of them scurrying to and fro with their striped backs and bushy tails. She took out her little automatic Canon (it was the last camera we had that used film), and, with her back firmly turned on the spectacular orange-pink vista that stretched out behind her, she took picture after picture of these modest little creatures.

Los Angeles is America's America; we drove down Interstate 5, which follows the Central Valley as it turns from slightly green to dry, brown, and harsh before climbing over the mountains and depositing its load of vehicles into the thick web of highways that crisscrosses the vast metro-sea. For her, that first trip was like a voyage to Mars. But she would grow to love LA. We had a barbecue, for which we purchased a tiny grill made in China, on which were printed the words, "This is not a Weber." How she laughed at that. And what did we grill? Not a hamburger in sight: *melanzane, peperoni, zucchine* (eggplants, peppers, zucchini). She taught me how to sweat the eggplants and put them under oil with a little mint, and how to burn the skin off the peperoni (that is, red bell peppers) and then cut them into thin slices to put them under oil *con un po' di aglio* (with a little garlic). We were already building that combination of the two cultures that was so much a part of us.

History

We had returned to Rome in the late summer of 2000. The tall windows in her luminous, high-ceilinged corner office were opened onto the Via Venti Settembre; it was a crystalline late-autumn day, and Emanuela was behind her desk, which was covered with *cartelle* (folders) and archival boxes of various sorts. She exercised an easy authority at the Tavola Valdese: careful, competent, and very intelligent. She was by far the youngest employee but had one of the most important positions: inspecting and authorizing the funding of grant proposals that came in from all over the world. Her boss was friendly enough, although I found his mild paternalism grating.

I occasionally met her there for lunch or to *prendere un caffè* (to get an espresso). The pausa caffè always took place in the kitchen off the office's main corridor. Everyone would come in, and Alba, one of the many aunt-like figures who orbited Emanuela, would put on the *caffettiera* (the coffee pot): an ancient Bialetti Moka stained black by years of use. The *tazzine* (espresso cups) were brought out on a tray with *zucchero* (sugar), and the coffee was carefully distributed in exactly equal quantities. Miraculously, there always seemed to be enough for the number of cups. Sometimes we would eat lunch there. There was a bustling and chaotic little place directly below the building that had *piadine* (flat, pita-like bread) with mortadella and sold *rosette* (rose-shaped bread rolls), which were her favorite. When I was feeling especially brave and competent with my Italian, I would sometimes go there myself and bring the rosette up to her office.

On that day, Emanuela was a bit distracted. "Vieni Dylan, guarda cosa sta succedendo!" (Look and see what's happening!) There were images of the 2000 presidential election in the

US—what seemed like groups of frat boys beating on bulletproof glass, harried election officials trying to figure out "hanging chads," excited CNN reporters. For her it was a bit disconcerting, I think. Despite my best efforts to disabuse her of this notion, she still had the idea that America was a kind of model of what a functioning democracy, and indeed a functioning society, might look like. The seedy underbelly was now being broadcast across the world, and available to everyone on the internet.

I had explained that elections in the US were run at the very local level, and that the entire machinery was opaque, antiquated, and riven with corruption. But this reality stood at such odds with the image of America as the paragon of political and social modernity that, at times, it seemed not to sink in. "Come è possibile che non possono contare i voti?" (How is it possible that they can't count the votes?) The hard lesson in the reality of "Democracy in America" was just beginning.

We spent a lot of time in the weeks after the US elections making the final preparations for our marriage. I had to purchase a suit, a simple charcoal thing, and she her elegant salmon-pink silk dress. There were numerous visits to "Rinascente," a department store near where Nonna Angiola lived.

(Emanuela and I had gone there before to buy underwear. For her I think this was a sign of us being a couple, but it was also because she had been horrified, as she later told me, to discover that I had holes in mine; she asked my advice on which ones looked nicest for her, and we decided on the Cacharel brand with little blue and white squares all over it and a small silk flower sewn on the waistband in the front. For me, she picked out a pair of *intimissimi*: I think they were red plaid.)

It was necessary to establish a registry: a list from which friends and family are supposed to purchase wedding gifts. The nascent marriage, in this way, comes to seem like a startup company, requiring an initial outlay of fixed capital in the form of domestic goods. I had wanted to select most of the things from the "Alessi" line, first because their whimsical designs seemed most in keeping with who we were, and second because one of the first gifts I bought her was a pepper mill and pepper shaker from their store in Milan. When it came to pots and pans, however, I was shot down because of the obvious superiority of the German competitor.

I remember a long and tedious afternoon spent with Sandra, Emanuela's mother, and an overenthusiastic salesperson in the basement of Rinascente, who described the German pots as "il Mercedes della cucina" (the Mercedes of the kitchen); she was particularly insistent on showing us how they could be stacked one inside the other, unlike the Alessi ones, which were somewhat rounded.

We also chose plates and *sottopiatti* (underplates). I had never even heard of this last item, and am still puzzled about its use. For both of us it seemed bizarre: we had no real place to live, no certainty about what continent we would be on, but many, many dishes. (Most of these remain to be unpacked, the hopeful promise of a house we never had.) The most useful items on our registry were the *valigie* (the suitcases) that Gianni gave us: the indestructible green hard-plastic luggage set that I still use. I'm not sure anyone thought we would make it except for us.

There was also the matter of the rings; I remember very clearly the day we got them. There are rainstorms in Rome where it seems like a giant waterfall has suddenly opened over the city. Rivers come pouring out of the sky, and the San Pietrini (cobblestones) become slick and treacherous; the fragile and ancient infrastructure seems to buckle under the weight of it all. It was on such a day that we picked up the rings. I remember the golden light coming out of the windows of the *gioielleria* (jeweler) and splashing down onto the dark paving stones. The rings themselves were perfect—simple, beautiful pieces with our names and the date of our marriage. I was only ever without mine for a few hours, when it fell off my finger at our house in Berkeley years later (around 2012). Emanuela searched for it furiously in the yard. Somehow, she found it. Her will was so strong that she could perform miracles like that.

In Italy, marriage is surrounded with much more bureaucratic formality than in the US. Firstly, it must be recorded in the official registry office, the *anagrafe*, which contains a list of all persons living in a particular area together with their civil status. The office is an extremely important institution since it serves as the basis for electoral rolls and the distribution of health and pension benefits. Anagrafi are mostly the product of the Napoleonic period and are built on systems of secular, not religious, population registration stretching back to antiquity. In any case, we had to provide a series of documents: a passport, visa, and a thing called a *nulla osta*, an official declaration that there existed no legal impediment to us marrying. This required several visits to the American embassy. I don't recall Emanuela having to do much, as she was already of course on the population rolls, and they had her key information.

When the documents were ready, we had to make a trip to the *questura* (police prefecture) with two witnesses. These were Mario and Patrizia. (I had come to understand in the meantime that she had a quasi-familial relationship with them that was very important to her. Relations broke down years later because we didn't spend enough time with them on one of our visits to Rome from the US. I never understood this break. It remains for me an inscrutable *italianata*, an Italian affair.) Each questura serves a particular area of the *municipio* (city government), and we had to go to the one near Fonte Meravigliosa, the neighborhood where Emanuela grew up. It was a grim building. There was much declaring, signing of forms, and stamping of documents. At that point there were no obstacles to us being legally married in the eyes of *lo stato* (the state), but we left the final formality for the wedding.

The ceremony itself was held in a deconsecrated church, the Chiesa di Santa Maria in Tempulo, which sits directly across from the giant ancient baths complex, the Terme di Caracalla. We sat in two huge golden thrones while an official from the *comune* (municipality) wearing a large sash (the *assessore culturale*, the cultural commissioner) droned out bureaucratic formulae that I barely understood. I said "Sì" at the appropriate time, as did she, and we were married.

Outside there was a swirling milieu of Americans and Italians blinking in the sunlight; they were slightly dazed and quite unable to communicate among themselves. It was absolutely lovely.

Afterward there was a reception at Emanuela's friend Alessia's hotel in EUR. Our wedding cake was a *millefoglie* (mille-feuille) topped with two little blonde wedding figurines who bore no resemblance to us at all. Prosecco flowed, people ate; there was even some speechifying, and lots of poorly understood communication between English speakers and Italians.

From a bureaucratic perspective, we had made a fundamental error by marrying in Italy, and we compounded it by starting the immigration process only after we had wed. What we should have done is apply for a temporary visa to the US for the purposes of marrying there. As a result of our mistake, we got a bit entangled in the exhausting and expensive American immigration bureaucracy, which, as anyone who has had any contact with the euphemistically named Immigration and Naturalization Service (now the US Citizenship and Immigration Services) knows, is exquisitely designed to dehumanize, degrade, and bankrupt those who must have dealings with it.

The upshot of our bureaucratic ineptitude was that she would have to wait in Italy, and this meant more separation for us. I remember once walking together near the Porta San Pancrazio. She was very angry with me. Her eyes flashed as she asked, "Com'è possibile che non hai iniziato la pratica?" (How can you not have started the case?) In reality the question wasn't entirely fair. We had procrastinated together. But she had a fear that something was going to tear us apart. It was as if she felt that what we had was too beautiful to last, and that we must take special care to protect it.

She always wore a chain with the embossed image of a little angel hanging from it. "Che cos'è?" (What is it?) I asked. "È il mio angelo protettore" (It's my guardian angel), she said. I asked her never to take it off; that way it would always protect her. I'm wearing it now.

The afternoon of September 11, 2001, I was out browsing through magazines and newspapers at a *giornalaio* (a newspaper stand)* when Emanuela called and told me I needed to return immediately home because there had been some sort of attack. The portiere evidently had been frantically asking where I was; I guess I was the only americano that he knew. His worry was completely irrational, but also endearing in a way. I remember sitting on the couch watching our tiny TV when the second of

---

* These wonderful little stalls were still ubiquitous in the early 2000s but have become much less common now. The ones that have survived pervasive digitalization are now almost exclusively devoted to selling tourist knickknacks.

the two towers collapsed. We both knew immediately that this was a major watershed. The easygoing late-nineties world of travel would come to a screeching halt, replaced by paranoia and bureaucracy. Emanuela was more shaken than I at the time.

Only a couple of days later, we had to fly to England where I had been invited to participate in a conference with my advisor, the sociologist Michael Mann. Flying always made her slightly nervous, and the attack accentuated this. I argued that we were probably quite safe given that the likelihood of two attacks in the space of a couple of days was very small. But she was a bit agitated. She had also not been to England (which she referred to as *la perfida Albione*, the perfidious Albion) before. Her main experience with English people was with the beer-sodden football fans who would occasionally descend on Rome like a Vandalic horde. We landed in "Cool Britannia" at the height of Tony Blair's popularity, before his disastrous backing of the second Iraq War. We had to take a bus from Heathrow to Cambridge, passing through the English countryside; Emanuela was charmed by the farmhouses and the gently undulating greenery of the landscape.

The conference organizers put us up in a room on the campus, which was comfortable enough but had a bizarrely configured bathroom; the shower head protruded directly above the toilet instead of being mounted in a separate area, and there was of course no bidet. She shook her head. "Sti inglesi sono ridicoli." (These English are ridiculous.)

The afternoon of our arrival we walked around Cambridge a bit. We noted the immaculate lawns reserved only for professors of a certain status, and both laughed at the absurd medievalisms of the place. At one point she wanted to buy cigarettes. She was still smoking a bit at the time. We walked to a gas station near the campus. The cashier, after I had paid, asked me if I was an American. When I responded affirmatively, he handed me a candle in memory of the victims of the attack on the Twin Towers; Emanuela was astonished by this. "Come hanno fatto a sapere?" (How did they know?), she asked me. This was the first time that she realized that English, like Italian, had different accents.

I remember the packets of euros that the Italian government sent around to everyone to introduce them to the new money, together with a helpful little calculator decorated with the now-ubiquitous European flag, for working out the exchange rate. For a couple of months there was *doppia circolazione* (double circulation): both euros and lire were in use. All the cashiers had two trays of money to make change. Everyone was trying to game the prices, to figure out what currency one should use. As the euro began to displace the lira, though, the reality of the situation sank in; prices doubled, and overnight we went from being comfortable to quite uncomfortable.

After our marriage but before I had finished my dissertation, which I completed in the summer of 2002, we were flying back and forth all the time from Los Angeles to Rome. I recall one arrival very clearly. I stepped off the plane bleary eyed and jet lagged: *bagagli*, *passaporto*, *la dogana* (baggage, passport, customs). Emerging through the doors at Fiumicino Airport into the waiting area near the taxi stand, I spotted Emanuela. Her jet-black hair was cut shoulder length, her flashing eyes embraced me even before we touched: all warmth and wool, and the smell of her skin. "Ti amo, amore. Benvenuto a casa." (I love you, my love. Welcome home.) It was then I realized that *casa* was not a place but was simply wherever she was.

Erba Alta

Tall pines and redwoods that, when the sun is out, dapple the road with disconcerting shadows, appearing sometimes as holes or puddles, surround the backroads from California's Napa Valley to the coast on which we were driving. It was just the two of us; it must have been late 2002 or early 2003. I had convinced her to take a trip to see the ocean. Emanuela at that time was a bit reluctant about such things, the whole idea of driving substantial distances for a picnic still foreign to her.

For our trip we had made *insalata di riso* (rice salad); the rice we used was arborio, and we put olive oil, *ciliegine* (mozzarella balls), tomatoes, olives, pickled vegetables, and capers in it. She packed it carefully in a little plastic container, and we brought some plates and knives from the house. The plan was to find a picnic table overlooking the water.

After an hour or so of driving, the winding road abruptly intersected the Pacific Coast Highway, and immediately the light, the air, and the scents changed. Instead of a shady forest, bright blue sky; instead of stuffy, close air, a cool saltwater breeze; and instead of pine, coastal lavender and sage. Her eyes lit up, and I saw her relax. It had been a difficult few months. Life in California was still so strange: all driving and sun and isolation. And she was missing things that she had never particularly noticed before: church bells, for example. The silence of the California days, and particularly the nights, was disquieting to her. It seemed empty, or perhaps completely false, as if we were in reality living on a giant stage set, like in *The Truman Show*. "È bellissimo" (It's beautiful), she said, taking in the expanse.

That, I think, was the first time she really registered the immensity of the Pacific, its horizon-gobbling blueness, the way people and their habitations seemed to shrink into insignificance beside its grandeur. We parked at a coastal access point from where we could see a small cluster of trees, seemingly huddled together for warmth against the wind, about a quarter mile from the car. I suggested that we walk toward them. Manu hesitated. The area between the car and the trees was covered by yellow grass that reached about halfway up our calves. She looked at the trees and then down at the grass. "Erba alta," she said. "Non mi piace." (Tall grass. I don't like it.)

She must have been told as a child that *erba alta* contained hidden dangers, likely snakes. I tried to convince her; I ran halfway out to the trees. "Guarda amore, non c'è niente" (Look love, there's nothing here); but she was rooted to the spot. There was no convincing her once she had made up her mind, so I relented. We drove a little way further up the coast and stopped at a lovely overlook to eat our insalata di riso. Years later, when she had become used to the wildness of the coast, she would laugh about "erba alta," thinking back, maybe with a touch of longing, to the woman she had been when she first set foot in this strange and wild land.

Shock

I had secured a teaching gig at the University of California, Davis, for a year, but applications for a permanent position had to be sent out, and I was trying to publish. We lived in Napa. It was lonely for her, and stressful for me. In a funny way, we still didn't really know each other; or, rather, we knew each other when she was the one with the full-time job and the native speaker of the language, and I was the student and non-native speaker. Now everything was reversed and upside down.

It was hard for both of us; I knew she was lonely and perhaps depressed. I was frustrated and angry with a market that yielded only a telephone interview at Mississippi State. Once, in a fit of rage, I threw a heavy roll of duct-tape against the drywall in the office, leaving a hole; my anger was out of control. She was horrified, I think. But she comforted me. "Sei bravo, sarà tutto OK" (You're capable, love, everything is going to be OK), she said. Then came the news, probably toward the end of February (we had moved to Davis in the meantime): an invitation to give a job talk at the Central European University in Budapest. (The place had been set up in the late nineties as a democracy-promotion project and a conduit for gifted students from the former Soviet world to get to the West; one of the great privileges of my time there was to be sociologist Volodymyr Ishchenko's teacher. Hungary's prime minister, Viktor Orbán, later shut down most of its operations and forced the staff to move to Vienna, where it still operates.)

My trip coincided with the criminal US assault on Iraq; the tanks were rolling as I flew. Partially because we did not have a TV at the time, and got our news exclusively from print media, neither of us could figure out why anyone believed the various stories swirling around about "weapons of mass destruction." It all seemed an obvious pretext.

We first went back to Rome before going on to Hungary. Emanuela was pregnant with Eamon, and it was hot. We decided to take the train to Budapest since she felt more comfortable doing that than flying. I remember only images of the trip, like old photographs in my memory: the station at Trieste (the last stop in Italy), the innumerable passport checks as we wended our way through the former Yugoslavia; the arrival in Hungary with its squat-green electrical towers and low-gray sky. "Dove mi hai portato?" (Where have you brought me?) she asked, half-jokingly. We had a brief conversation with the railway conductor, who was deeply nostalgic for the good old days of "Goulash Communism" under comrade János Kádár. We arrived at Keleti station at midmorning and began life in Hungary, where I had finally secured a job.

It felt like we were living again, growing together, building a life together. The weird parenthesis of the year at Davis was quickly fading. It helped that we had such a beautiful apartment on Ülloi Utca in Pest, rented from a colleague at the CEU, Béla Greskovits. It had high ceilings, wooden floors, striking, tall windows that let in as much light as there was to be had, and a massive ceramic stove that provided heat to the whole apartment.

Capitalism had definitely established itself, but there were certain peculiarities for those coming from the "West," as we did. If one wanted to buy food from the local grocery store, it was essential to arrive well before noon, as nothing much was left after that—or, rather, nothing except for extremely old and suspect canned goods. Part of our salary was paid directly in food coupons, so we rarely paid in cash for groceries; in general, consumption was simpler and more modest than in either Italy or, of course, the US.

When we arrived, Emanuela was exactly halfway through her pregnancy, so we had a chance to compare prenatal care in Davis and Budapest. The contrast was stark. In Davis the care was bureaucratic, perfunctory, and expensive. In Hungary it was personalized, thorough, and (even accounting for the "tips" we were expected to leave) extremely cheap. Emanuela quickly adapted to the new life and by the end of the second month was a known quantity in our neighborhood, although no one could exactly decide who she was. An Italian? A Palestinian refugee? An American?

The day we arrived in Budapest, I put the application in the mail for the job at Berkeley. Personally, I had little hope that anything would come of it, but she encouraged me to send it on anyway; I promptly forgot about it. This was neither the first nor the last time she showed more belief in me that I did in myself. Life unfolded. When we couldn't find pasta at the grocery store (surprisingly common), we made *maltagliati* (handmade noodles) with ragù.

Birth

I traveled to the US a little over two weeks before Eamon was born. Emanuela's father, Matteo, was there when I arrived back, but there had been a gap when she had been alone. This seems inexcusable to me now, but at the time I felt that I had no choice.

There must have been six or eight women in the spotlessly clean room with polished floors and painted steel beds. Anxious husbands attended to their very pregnant wives. She wanted something to eat, and nothing was open. Luckily, it being the end of history, there was a McDonald's, and our last pre-Eamon meal was a delicious order of Hungarian chicken nuggets.

Eamon came into the world with a full head of hair that started basically at his eyebrows. His entire forehead was covered with a thick fuzz: *pelosetto*. They whisked him away after the C-section and placed him under an orange heat lamp, next to an extremely fair-skinned Hungarian baby. I looked at both, a study in contrasts, and imagined what completely different lives awaited each. "Welcome to the world," I said. Then I rushed back to Emanuela; they were moving her to the recovery ward; she felt cold, and I was frightened. But she quickly regained her strength as they fed her celery root soup, and I spent the rest of the morning shuttling between mother and child.

The red-brick Semmelweis Klinikák where Eamon was born seems a bit like a baby factory. I remember walking its halls, light streaming in through the enormous windows off the main corridor; strong-armed, white-clad nurses marched around the hospital with swaddled charges under each arm. The nursery itself resembled a bakery, with wooden shelves holding babies instead of bread.

Our "tip" had paid for a single room right next to the nursery. They brought Eamon to us in a little plastic bin on wheels; he had huge hands. (Later, when he started playing cello, Manu would always say, looking at his baby pictures, "Mani di un violoncellista!" Hands of a cellist!) Emanuela held him for a while, but that first night she was grateful when the nurses took him back. What neither of us knew was how little sleep was coming.

Eamon's arrival drew us inward and together like a gravitational force. Getting him to nurse, making sure he was warm, searching for the innumerable necessities and pseudo-necessities of infancy. Practical problems emerged. How does one say "diaper" in Hungarian?

There were many trips to IKEA, which was in the inner suburbs on the metro-line. The solid Russian-made trains trundled under Kerepesi Street, depositing our small family at an enormous square surrounded on three sides by giant Soviet-looking buildings, and on the fourth by the blue and yellow box that everywhere serves as a sign of Scandinavian consumer culture. There we bought, among many other things, his first bathtub: a blue plastic affair that he loved splashing around and peeing in. Exhaustion set in, of course: the universal experience of parenthood. For the first time we really learned to appreciate sleep and got little of it.

Eamon was born on December 9, just a couple of weeks before
Christmas. Budapest is a magical place during the holidays. I
remember wandering around our neighborhood near Kálvin
tér: the streets were full of artisans peddling clothes and toys. I
got a boiled-wool hat for Emanuela that framed her face very
well. For Eamon I found a wooden puzzle depicting a mother
elephant surrounding a baby. I wandered into the Vásárcsar-
nok, the market hall, with its vaulted ceiling, hanging lights,
and paprika. At Christmas time the entire place was festooned
with piglets hanging from rafters. It was at once horrifying and
weirdly festive.

As winter gave way to spring, we began to venture out more:
noi tre (the three of us). She was now known and loved in the
neighborhood. Everywhere we went, the middle-aged women
who staffed the stores would look at Eamon and congratulate
his mother. "Nagyon, nagyon szép" (Very, very beautiful), they
would say. "Köszönöm szépen" (Thank you), Emanuela would
reply.

One day, walking along the Danube, we came across a park
full of pensioners with their cats in cat carriers. They were taking
them outside to get their daily dose of vitamin D from the sun;
I had read somewhere that Budapest has the fewest sunny days
of any large city in the world.

Hungary's capital combined twin cities whose social and political geographies are closely related. The Pest side, where we
lived, is flat, full of apartment buildings, and historically the locus
of the working class, artists, Jews, and Roma. The Buda side is
on a massive hill full of dour stone mansions. It is a remnant of
the old Europe, Black aristocratic Europe—the Europe the Red
Army ended forever. We took trips there occasionally. From Buda
Castle looking out over the city and to the Tisza plain beyond, it

is hard not to imagine the last stand of the Nazis' Waffen-SS as Stalin's T-34 tanks inexorably pushed forward; it helps that the buildings are still scarred by machine-gun fire.

But the castle district is also quite picturesque; Emanuela had found an excellent pastry shop that served a delicious Eszterházy torte.* We once took a trip deep into Buda, on a tram that must have been built in the twenties, in search of a restaurant that was reputed to have the best Hungarian food in the city. The restaurant was excellent, but we were struck by the realization that "Hungarian cuisine," perhaps like many other aspects of Hungarian national identity, was a cultural project of the Eszterházy family and, like many other "national peculiarities," was mostly, and paradoxically, an imitation of a Gallic original. The meal, with its savory crêpes and rich sauces, was a Magyar translation from some nineteenth-century French cookbook.

Return

The final news must have come in January. My interview and talk, very much to my surprise, had gone over well, and thus I was being offered a permanent position. We were headed back to the US, this time to Berkeley. After the initial euphoria, a sadness overtook both of us, but especially Emanuela. There were many advantages to Budapest; it's a wonderful city with a highly cultivated, warm people who speak a beautiful and mysterious language. Public transportation is excellent, and the café culture recalls the best parts of the old empire. But, perhaps most importantly, it was culturally foreign to both of us. For the first and only time in our marriage, we were equidistant from the

---

* The Eszterházys were the greatest landholding family in Hungary prior to the Communist period.

circumambient society: immigrants both. The move back to the States would upset this balance once again.

Like the trip to Hungary some ten months before, the move back started with a train ride and was punctuated by a stopover in Rome. This time we decided to take the more northerly route that runs through Austria and enters Italy north of Milan. The gentle rocking of the cars as we wound through the Tirolese Alps put Eamon to sleep almost immediately. It seemed to us miraculous, as he had never slept more than two or three hours since he was born. I looked at the two of them; in infancy he was a carbon copy of his mom. They were all a mass of black hair and soft olive skin, resting peacefully. I wished we would never have to get off.

The *nonni* (grandparents) were overjoyed with Eamon but sad, as well, that we would once again be a continent and a half away. Emanuela was particularly stunning that summer on the terrazzo of the house at Via Riccardo Forster: her hair covered in a red bandana and her face lit up by the bronze Roman sun, her dark eyes flashing. She looked like some ferociously alluring partisan—one of those machine-gun-toting Italian women with their hair tied back who one sees in old pictures from the end of the Second World War.

Our first house in Berkeley, which we moved into in the early fall of 2004, was off Upper Solano on Ensenada Avenue. The place was comfortable, and indeed actually large for us. We had never had so much room. But we couldn't really afford the rent, and the space was disconcerting to us both. Although my salary had doubled, the difference in cost of living between Budapest and Berkeley left us distinctly poorer. Berkeley's underdeveloped system of public transportation was also a problem as we had no car. This, together with the demands of mothering an infant, isolated Emanuela during this first period.

The first months are a blur. I remember meeting my dear friend Sandra Smith, who joined Berkeley sociology that fall as well; although we didn't become immediately close, we had a similar reaction to the inane orientation for new faculty held in the Lipman Room at Barrows Hall; the building in which the sociology department is housed.* This was one of those events that universities feel obligated to put on, in which administrators read aloud information from printed material; the coup de grâce was when they tried to teach us the "Cal Fight Song." I fidgeted and squirmed until I was finally able to make my exit during a lull in these dreary proceedings.

I remember trying to put together a lecture on *The German Ideology* in the kitchen at the house on Ensenada on very little sleep; I had not read the text closely since probably my second year of graduate school. This was when I truly learned that crucial professorial skill, *parlare a braccio* (speaking off the cuff), as the Italians say, as the only thing I had time to produce was a crude diagram.

The early period in Berkeley was difficult for both of us. I felt the pressures of gaining tenure all the more as I had uprooted Emanuela three times, we had now landed in California, and of course there was Eamon. But she needed more help at home, and I was trying desperately to carve out time to write in the office. (A disastrous attempt to arrange an au pair from Italy did nothing but create more work.) I think this was probably the only time

---

* Neither name has survived: the Lipman room was demolished in a misconceived renovation project, and Barrows Hall was renamed the Social Sciences Building after David Prescot Barrows's long public record of racist paternalism toward the Philippines became a PR problem for a university that has no qualms about having a Bechtel Engineering Center and McCone Hall; the latter two men were both rabid anticommunists profoundly implicated in the worst US imperialist adventures from the overthrow of Iran's Mosaddegh on.

she seriously considered leaving me. She locked herself in the bathroom and yelled, "Non mi piace qui, non mi piace Berkeley, e sono stufa del tuo lavoro. Sono sempre da sola!" (I don't like it here, I don't like Berkeley, and I'm sick of your job. I'm always alone!) The words cut me to the quick, and I broke down. It was the most serious crisis of our marriage.

The move to the Clark Kerr Apartments eased our situation somewhat. The rent was less, there was a kind of ready-made community, and Eamon was growing. The restricted world of infancy broadened. This was when we began to discover the Bay Area through the experiential framework of a small child: the steam train in Tilden Park, the Bay Area Discovery Museum, libraries, the "negozio Thomas" (the store Eamon and Emanuela named after the Thomas the Tank Engines that were available in it) on College Avenue. Emanuela kept a diary of Eamon's first words, which were uttered in that apartment. When he wanted something he would say, "Asa oi," repeating as best he could his mamma's question, "Cosa vuoi?" (What do you want?)

It was during this time, too, that Nonna Sandra came to visit, spring of 2006: an odd experience in many ways. She suffered from some combination of terrible jetlag and culture shock. I remember that we took her to the Marin Headlands and to Napa. But I think it was fundamentally all just too enormous, too wild, and too foreign for her. She has not been back to the United States since. I think this hurt Emanuela very deeply, although she never quite let on how much.

When Eamon turned two years and nine months old, he was eligible for preschool (*asilo nido*, Emanuela called it). We found an excellent place in the basement of St. John's Church on College Avenue called Monterverde (also the name of the neighborhood of our second apartment in Rome). When we dropped him off the first day, Emanuela wanted to stay to do *adattamento*, a practice of parental waiting around that her friends back in Italy were talking about. But Eamon, who has never particularly lacked self-confidence, wasn't interested in that at all: he pushed us gently toward the gate and waved us goodbye before turning to plunge into the business at hand. Emanuela was a bit nonplussed, but I pointed out that his self-confidence was partly the product of how well she had mothered him up to that point.

At Monteverde, Eamon made his first friend, Nathaniel. "Playdates" and children's parties began. Emanuela initially found these affairs off-putting. Their informality, with children grabbing food and eating in a haphazard way, while the parents hovered together uncomfortably, usually in a kitchen or backyard, left her puzzled.

The neglect of the adults seemed particularly odd to her. These poor souls typically formed a random assemblage, thrown together by the accident of their children's friendships and left to fend for themselves sans either of the two great social lubricants: alcohol and caffeine. Thus, weekend mornings were often passed in awkward tedium. I think she found this strange and barbaric. But she adapted for the sake of her son, and quickly was able to enliven things, often by raising the culinary level a couple of notches with a *torta* (cake) of some sort.

What kind of mother was Emanuela in these early years? The love that she lavished on her son cannot be captured with adjectives. One has to say what she did. Let's begin with clothing. First of all, from the time he was born, Eamon was always impeccably dressed, until he began to make his own, occasionally questionable, sartorial decisions in high school. Even when he was a toddler, she would change his onesies (they are called *bodies* in Italian, one of those weird pseudo-English expressions that pollute that otherwise-beautiful language) multiple times a day so that he was amazingly clean.

She also attended carefully to his diet. We bought a "baby-food maker," which was basically a small blender. She would boil chicken breast and zucchini and then blend them together *con olio* (only the kind made with 100 percent Italian olives, a different and more restrictive designation than "Italian olive oil") and *parmigiano* (only *reggiano*, and only the fresh type, not the old fragments that sometimes appear at grocery stores).

Finally, he had an incredibly regular sleeping schedule: two naps, one in midmorning and the other after lunch. Perhaps because of Emanuela's style of parenting, Eamon never threw a tantrum and was almost never sick. It also gave him, paradoxical as this might sound, a supreme self-confidence and independence (as the first day at Monteverde showed). One of the many things that Emanuela taught me is that love and connection are not the opposite of freedom and self-determination, but rather their precondition.

The first visit to the doctor's office with Eamon revealed the chasm between American styles of parenting and what she thought appropriate. The Berkeley kids in the waiting room were all wearing clothes that resembled more or less shapeless and more or less clean cotton sacks, designed for ease and comfort. Eamon, in contrast, was dressed in an undershirt (*canottiera*), a button-up shirt (*camicia*), a stylish sweater-vest (*gilet*), and good-looking corduroys (*bei pantaloni di velluto*). He looked just like a miniature version of his very handsome grandfather when he had been younger. Dr. King, Eamon's pediatrician with whom we would later become close, and whose sons are now among Eamon's best friends, was flustered. Used to slipping off onesies or, at most, pulling up a shirt, he faced in Eamon an elegant little onion that had to be peeled layer by layer. Afterward, when we had dinner with the Kings, we would often laugh together and remember that first visit.

Insegnante (Teacher)

Emanuela had dreamed of becoming a historian. Her tesi di laurea, written under the direction of Giuseppe Parlato, a student of Renzo De Felice, with whom Emanuela had also studied, is an archivally rich investigation of the use of Mazzinian imagery in the propaganda of the Repubblica di Salò. It was through her connection to Parlato that she had initially secured a position at the Fondazione Spirito, of which he was the director. But there were difficulties, above all the entrenched male dominance of the history profession in Italy.

The problem was evident in microcosm in the gendered division of labor at the Fondazione. The researchers who came to consult the documents, as well as the Fondazione's leadership, were overwhelmingly men. The staff, in contrast, was made up entirely of women. It was my impression that Emanuela had initially taken the job with the hope that it might be an entrée into academic life. But it had later become obvious that Parlato viewed her primarily as an office worker. It was clear, however, that the Fondazione's leadership relied heavily on her competence and intelligence. On at least one occasion, she essentially composed an essay for the foundation's *Annali* (an annual) out of the less than fully coherent musings of an elderly professor who had spoken at a conference. To produce the piece required her not only to transcribe the written remarks, but to then edit them together into something like a coherent piece: no small feat. (The practice of publishing what are often extemporaneous speeches is much more widespread in Italian intellectual life than in the Anglosphere.)

When Emanuela came to the US, it was partially with the idea that she might pursue graduate school. Both of us, I think, underestimated the difficulties, both emotional and cultural, of being an immigrant. In our early years together, our peripatetic existence exacerbated these challenges. As Eamon grew, Emanuela reinvented herself as a teacher of Italian. She threw herself into the work. (For one of her classes, I clearly remember helping her put together an extensive slide show covering each of the regions of Italy, with units on culture, art, history, and cuisine.)

She would always try to convey in her teaching a sense of the history of her country, especially its more recent history (say, from 1871 onward). I think to some extent she saw herself as a cultural ambassador, tasked particularly with breaking the superficial romanticism to which many Americans are in thrall with regard to Italy. "Gli americani pensano solo a pizza, pasta, e mandolino, quando pensano all'Italia" (Americans think only of pizza, pasta, and mandolins when they think about Italy), she would say. Of course, more than most, I benefited from her intelligence and learning. Emanuela read, commented on, and edited virtually everything I wrote, saving me from countless errors. As she became more confident with English, she offered acute substantive and stylistic suggestions. She also developed a simple and powerful style in English, one most evident in her final blog postings.

Consider, for example, this one, describing a day at the cancer center just eight months before her passing.

Another Friday, another infusion, another day in the Precision Cancer Center at UCSF Mission Bay. I got back home a couple of hours ago, exhausted but ok. Infusion day doesn't always start at the same time. Today was early. We dropped off Eamon at school (his last junior day of in-person instruction) and then we drove to UCSF. Finding parking was a challenge; but we finally found a spot on the 8th floor of the parking garage. We used the stairs instead of the elevator and I already knew that my blood pressure was going to be higher than usual. Anyway, for some reason that we don't clearly understand, they let Dylan through the Covid checkpoint so he could be with me in the waiting room. Life on the 4th floor starts with a check in for the blood draw; after that you wait for your turn. Once they call my name, the nurse in the blood room accesses my port—it's in a weird position, and for this reason everyone remembers me. Soon after the blood draw, we wait till the results are in, and Dylan is still around because we learned our lesson. Once it happened that Dylan left me before the blood draw and got back to Berkeley. The results were not good and so they cancelled my chemo. Poor Dylan had to drive back to SF to pick me up! Anyway, today the blood results were good. So, I said goodbye to Dylan and went into the infusion area. I walked to my assigned chair and soon after my nurse arrived with the pre-medicine (a combination of anti-nausea, steroids, and hydration drugs). Today I did not get the room with a view, and I did not get my favorite nurses; but Teresa was good and with a witty sense of humor. My 3 room companions were no fun —3 men—with no social skills! Lol I'm very demanding. During the infusion I normally knit (what a shocker!) or listen to my dear Eamon playing music. Sometimes I fall asleep . . . I finished my infusion, they attached my chemo pump and I went back home. I'm now resting waiting for dinner and maybe a movie with Dylan (Eamon is going back to school for a junior night event). Thanks to everyone who brought us food, or came to walk and knit with me this week. Have a great weekend everyone. Love you all!

Appreciation for the nurses, worry about me having to drive back across the bridge, an observation on the poor social skills of her chemo-mates, the determination in the face of all this to keep knitting, and her incredible bravery in the face of terrible circumstances; it is so typical of her, and so directly and clearly expressed. Perhaps most characteristic is her careful thanking of everyone, from the nurses to our friends who were giving us so much support at the time.

This raises a painful question. What was coming next for Emanuela as Eamon grew? Would she have realized her dream of becoming a historian, or rather would she have emerged as an artist, or would she have continued teaching? Among many things, Emanuela was a promise tragically unfulfilled. It is for this, too, perhaps for this above all, that I grieve.

Lezioni di cultura politica

Emanuela taught me much of the grammar of Italian politics; and her own views naturally shifted as she began to learn that of the US. The central issue of her own country during most of our marriage could be summarized in a single word: Berlusconi. What did she make of this phenomenon, especially when considered through the prism of her new circumstances? One reading of course was paternalism, il Cavaliere as the *buon padre di famiglia* (good family man); the other was the peculiar appeal that cleverness has in Italian culture, and from this perspective Berlusconi was a *furbacchione* (a sly fox); a third perspective was the naive cynicism that so many of her fellow Italians express toward politics per se, *sono tutti ladri* (they are all thieves). Then there was the over-the-top masculinity, particularly apparent in the "bunga bunga" scandal, when Berlusconi's relations with underage prostitutes became the focus of media attention. We had many conversations about how to understand him, especially in the context of her trying to convey a sense of the country's politics to her students.

What became apparent to both of us was how unsatisfying any analysis based on cultural peculiarities was. We concluded that Berlusconi's appeal was rooted in two quite mundane realities. First, he was a very effective salesman of what was basically a US model of good life: material abundance, plenty of bad TV, and a depoliticized public sphere. Second, he promised to cut taxes—high taxes paid to a state offering relatively little in the way of effective public services. While never denying *berlusconismo*'s specifically Italian character, she would grow very impatient with the temptation, manifested in some of her students, and in much of the US media, to explain him in terms of national stereotypes. Trump's election, about which she was quite disturbed, gave her a certain sense of satisfaction in this way, for it rendered absurd the question, "How can the Italians vote for that man?"

We did not agree on everything regarding Italian politics. Paradoxically she saw the Movimento 5 Stelle (Five Star Movement) in much more anthropological terms than she did Berlusconi, and she judged it negatively. It was the expression, she thought, of a vulgar ignorance dismayingly widespread among those about a half generation younger than her. I tended to see it as a more progressive phenomenon: supportive of basic income, for example, and with a healthy disdain for the Italian political establishment, but she would have absolutely none of it.

She had an evolving and rather complex view of the US. Like many Europeans, and Americans for that matter, she was quite struck by Obama's election. She saw it as a manifestation of a very attractive feature of US culture, what she called *rispetto* (respect). In her understanding, one of the biggest differences between Italy and the US was that in the latter culture there was a kind of default assumption that persons in themselves are worthy of acknowledgment, while in the former, casual disdain, especially for one's appearance (which could take the form of racism or body shaming), was widely accepted. It's important to note in this regard that Emanuela's gender played a role in how she interpreted her adopted country; she simply felt freer as a woman in the US than she did in Italy.

That did not prevent her from finding the prissy self-righteousness of the Bay Area upper-middle classes stifling and absurd. The racial affinity groups that Eamon was expected to be a part of in high school were mysterious to her; she was frustrated by being continually miscoded as a Latina.

Blessedly Quotidian

The days of our first years in Berkeley went rolling by in a whirl of love and care. There were the birthday cakes for Eamon; the first one we made was in the shape of a car. She had purchased the cake mold, and we were up past midnight icing it with little blue flowers. There were the notes she hid in my luggage when I went on a trip, usually to some conference or other. They gave me strength, especially in those early years when every presentation seemed so fraught.

There were the lunch bags that she made; they were sewn with oil cloth inside so they could be easily wiped out. Then, of course, there were the lunches themselves, which we both made, but up to her standard. This meant no sandwiches, and certainly no PB and J's, the common meal for American grade-schoolers. Instead, Eamon had *pasta con sugo*, *pasta con pesto*, or *minestrone* (pasta with red sauce, pasta with pesto, vegetable soup), which he carried in a little green thermos that we had purchased at Target years before. There was the time that she bought letter molds that we used to cut out cheddar cheese, either with the letters of his name or "ti amo," or sometimes both.

There was dropping Eamon off at Thousand Oaks (his elementary school) and reading to him and his tablemates. There were the letters and notes that I wrote to Emanuela during the day, less often, really, than I should have, but not infrequently. There were the phone calls half a dozen times a day. I still have the last ones on my answering machine at the office. "Amore, chiamami quando puoi." (Love, call me when you can.) There were the trips to the coast—to Abbotts Lagoon, which she loved, and to eat oysters. There was the period when she volunteered with her friend Holli at the White Elephant Sale, an East Bay institution, and was quickly promoted to the sewing department. There was the job teaching at Italingua, a private language school—an experience that ended in some sordid Italianate backstabbing that I never fully grasped.

For a while Eamon and I would drop her off at the Flood Building (the same one where Amy and I had worked so many years before) in downtown San Francisco and we would explore the city—usually the area past Fisherman's Wharf, where there was an old sailboat, the *Balclutha*, and the maritime museum, both of which he loved.

There were Eamon's first cello lessons at the music house on Ashby with his teacher Sergei, who at first seemed impossibly austere but later became almost a member of our family. In those days, Eamon would go to the Jewish Community Center (JCC) on Walnut Street after school; I would pick him up at half past three for his lesson and whisk him across town after fueling him with a cupcake or a scone. When we came home, Manu would look at his clothes. "Sono così sporchi che li devo incenerire" (They are so dirty I need to incinerate them), she would say.

At the JCC Eamon was part of a Dungeons and Dragons club led by a young bearded undergraduate named Jake; later Emanuela hired him to be the "dungeon master" for his birthday at Ashkenaz, a social center and musical venue, on San Pablo Avenue.

There were the Mother's Days when we would buy her succulents at Cactus Jungle. After Eamon went to the Crowden School there were the concerts for which she would make elaborate platters of food: vegetables, hummus, ciliegine with tomatoes and pesto, and even a *frittata con piselli* (omelet with peas) cut into little rectangles to convert it into finger food. We developed a standardized shopping list of things to buy from Trader Joe's and Monterey Market for these occasions.

There was the period when she had her own studio space, which she shared with her friend Marina and where she made brightly colored handbags. I helped her to set up the space and often accompanied her to carry equipment and supplies up the steel-caged stairs outside the building.

There was the day she decided to start working at Avenue Yarns; I was worried it would take away time from what she really wanted to do, which was to create. But she insisted. "Abbiamo bisogno di soldi" (We need money), she said. There were all the times I brought her coffee or lunch or a snack to the store to get her through the day. There were the customers who loved her and sought out her advice. There were the times that I would walk her to the store in the morning; we would get a coffee at the HighWire, a café located inside the nursery across the street, and I would help her put the sign out when she opened the store.

There was the time the little red soft-serve ice cream truck, called "Brown Cap," which had a seal with a brown woolen hat painted on its side, parked across the street. She called me, and I came from working at home so we could get ice cream together. There were the lunches at the banh mi place on Lower Solano called Kim's. There were the times that I would make dinner when she came home late; she particularly liked the baked polenta dishes that I invented. (My main failure in this regard was that I could never really get her to enjoy mushrooms, which I thought were good for her.)

There were the mornings when I made pancakes with *sciroppo d'acero* (maple syrup)—the one thing she was never able to cook. Hers always came out flat and rubbery, halfway between a crêpe and a crumpet. "Uffa" (Damn), she would say. "Non hai il tocco americano" (You don't have the American touch), I would reply, which irritated her to no end.

There were the trips to the garden store in Richmond, and the time we grew tomatoes in terra-cotta planters (eventually we built a raised bed). There was playing nerf hoop with Eamon outside our kitchen, before he could enjoy a real court. There was the terrible day our cat Julius died, when she called me and I rushed home to hold him as he expired, and then buried him in our garden.

His death somehow marked for me the point of transition: the passing from quotidian bliss to chaos and darkness. Back pain, Trump, pandemic, cancer, Manu's death. Time has a double shape; it is divided into periods, and within each it is experienced differently. In those broad, sunny episodes, it flows by gently as things seem to be unfolding toward their predetermined goal; but then there are the periods of acceleration when it rushes by, as through a steeply descending tunnel that lets out into some unknown and quite other landscape.

Change of Tempo

It is just such a cascade that I need to convey now. Things suddenly quickened, shifted gear, and also slid off their appointed
course. The horizon darkened, and our future twisted itself into a
strange, sad, and foreshortened shape. But the tempo of the prose
must somehow invert this transformation to present it. The broad
melodies that covered years now give way to a tighter staccato:
less time and more prose.

Anniversary

The last real anniversary—real in the sense that Emanuela
was well and the world was relatively normal—that we spent
together was in 2019. We decided to walk across the Golden Gate
Bridge, something we had always wanted to do but hadn't the
time. Eamon was in school (he had begun his first year at Lick-
Wilmerding High School); it felt like the beginning of a new
chapter in our marriage: one in which we would do the things
that we had put off for years.

We parked on the Marin side of the bridge and donned our
woolen hats; she had made mine. The wind was cool and bracing,
and little wisps of fog were scudding across the span. Emanuela
was knitting as we walked: it was the blue cowl that she thought
looked good with my beard.

From a distance, or speeding past in a car, the bridge seems
clean and carefully painted. But up close, one witnesses the titanic
struggle between steel and saltwater. The reddish-orange rust-
proof paint that workers constantly apply is everywhere chipped
and cracked and buckling and bubbling. The sidewalk, made of
the same metal as the bridge itself, is pocked with holes through

which one can see the water of the bay as it churns through the Golden Gate. To the right, perilously close, a steady river of cars rushes by.

About halfway across, Emanuela put her knitting away, and we held close to one another as we proceeded. We were thoroughly chilled by the time we returned to the car, and we finished the day with cake from the little Hungarian pastry shop across the street from the Berkeley Bowl grocery store. It was one of those very modest, but very lovely, days that I appreciated at the time—but hardly enough, in the light of the terrible period to come.

Through Her Eyes

Emanuela created beauty through her way of being in the world. She bestowed it on things that she saw, and those things, in turn, lent theirs to her. She paid particular attention to small things, to humble things: the orange of California poppies, the purples and greens of lavender, the deep red-brown of the manzanita bark, the quaint shapes of succulents (*piante grasse*).

She would walk around the neighborhood collecting colors and shapes as she went about her daily routine; she would then pour all this collected beauty out again in the things that she made. The purples and the oranges and greens were turned into hats and scarves and fingerless gloves, so that we became, in a way, a reflection and recapitulation of the little slice of the world that was our own.

There were also the animals; dogs and cats, birds and squirrels were never to be passed by without a greeting. There was the rust-colored Maine coon who lived down Curtis Street, toward the BART tracks. There had initially been a pair, but one disappeared, a victim of a car or disease. That had saddened her, almost as if a dear friend had passed. There was "Bear," the Himalayan who lived on Rose just past the park. When she passed by, he always made the effort to lift his massive ursine form in greeting, requesting and receiving belly rubs and letting her proceed only with great reluctance.

Then there were the dogs: Mr. Tibbs, the odd-looking little creature who resembled the Lorax and who belonged to the parents of one of Eamon's classmates. There was Henry, the gray poodle, and flatulent little Freddie, the French bulldog; and of course, there was chocolate-colored Kaya, our neighbors' dog and perhaps the friendliest animal on earth. Emanuela made sure that all these beings were given their due, interacted with, appreciated. They were to be spoken with and examined. Did they seem well? Were they fatter or leaner than the last time she had passed?

When I go on my walks now, I try to see the world through her eyes—to attend to things in the way that she did, to collect images and colors. But of course, I don't have those gifts that she had—the color sense, the sense of the beauty of the small; but at least she let me see in ways that I had never seen before.

Do they feel neglected? What do the flowers make of her passing? Do the cats miss their belly rubs? It is hard to imagine that they do not. It is not just me; it is the whole neighborhood that feels flatter, less cared for, less regarded. It is an incomplete beauty longing for its audience.

Last Spring

Looking back, there were certain unmistakable signs: the pro-dromes of the coming disaster. For example, why was she so out of breath from walking up the stairs at the house of John and Jessica, my father and his wife, in McKinleyville? Why did she keep aspirating fluids? Why did she have abdominal pain? From the time that we were married, I was always at least a little worried about her health. For some reason, I connected her problems to the fact that she had been born prematurely. (She had had a sister, born some years before her, who also had been premature but did not survive. She is buried in Mantova.) But she continued to be active throughout the spring of 2020, the first of the COVID-19 pandemic; she sewed protective masks for everyone in the family after we moved up to Napa; we made bread and took walks, and she taught more than ever (now remotely).

We were still full of hope—although people who are full of hope don't quite know that they are until it is taken away. Among the hopes were these: that the pandemic would end quickly, surely by the fall; that whatever was bothering Emanuela physically would certainly be straightened out when she could see a physician in person; that we would be able to travel again soon.

There was also the fact that what was happening to her was simply inconceivable for me. Sometimes she had panic attacks; she intuited, I think, that something was seriously wrong. I saw it as my job to comfort her. "Sarà tutto OK, amore." (It will all be OK, love.) These were the words of a well-meaning ignoramus. I had always felt a profound responsibility to protect her, to ensure *che stava bene* (she was well). I wanted so much that her life be as beautiful as she, and I knew that she had faced many difficulties—her younger sister's illness, for example, and the sometimes strange behavior of her family.

I tried to give her what she needed, which I think came down to this: support without judgment. But I can't help feeling that I failed in the biggest and most basic thing. Wasn't I supposed, above all, to keep her safe? Wasn't I supposed to see when she was well and when she was ill, and in a sense before the doctors could make such determinations, since they didn't really know her?

When I look back at her pictures, I can see it now; I compare, for example, how she looked in 2015, bright eyes, dark shiny hair, healthy skin, to how she looked in 2019, tired and somehow swollen. Perhaps part of the problem was my very reluctance to judge her; to articulate the physical deterioration that I could see with my own eyes long before the diagnosis. That's how acceptance becomes betrayal and caring becomes neglect.

Cancer

Cancer is a pitiless dialectician. It turns strengths into weaknesses; it takes intimacy and makes of it an obstacle. It drains hope of its power and converts it into self-delusion; it uses growth to create death and destruction. It turns physical vitality into a debilitating illness. If evil ever could be thought of, against Augustine's teaching, as real, like the Manichaeans did, it would surely be cancer: a tangled, disordered growth, an anti-flourishing.

Is it irrational to hate a disease? No. Hatred in this case, as well as in the case of social ills (which seem to me to bear more than a passing similarity to cancers), sharpens one's thinking. Many of the people we met through Emanuela's illness seemed to me to hate the thing as much as I did. They had in fact dedicated their lives to its "defeat," which before this experience I had thought an odd expression in relation to a disease: an impermissible anthropomorphism.

Cancer also teaches this; however much the human species has already conquered "first nature," from the perspective of subsistence, there is still a virtually endless horizon of struggle against disease. Could it be that it is precisely here that capitalism still finds its greatest historical justification? Against all the many very obvious criticisms that can be made against the US "health care system" (a phrase in which the noun is very much in doubt) must be set the dynamic complex of venture capital and university expertise that, in the pursuit of profit, is constantly pushing at the frontier: immunotherapy, targeted radiation, combination therapies, and so on. Is it so obvious that the socialization of medical care would be able to maintain this dynamic?

But then again, what of the diseases themselves? To what extent is cancer, particularly colon cancer, itself a biomedical expression of capitalism's irrationality? When I asked her first oncologist, a friendly Russian man with an appreciation for cello playing, why she had been afflicted with this disease, his terse response was, "Western diet." In one sense that was absurd since Emanuela never really ate what might be considered a "Western diet"; it was mostly pasta, grains, olive oil, vegetables, and cheese. She ate very little meat. But in a more general sense I think the term must have indicated consumer capitalism.

Certainly Emanuela, especially when she was younger, ate, as "we" (meaning everyone born around 1970 or so) all have done, too many processed foods, too many things wrapped in plastic, too many food dyes, and so on. Colon cancer was an unwonted exception before the rise of mass packaging, with its deadly conveniences. In that sense it could be said that the capitalist "medico-industrial complex" dedicated to combating cancer arises from the same soil as the problem that defines it. Would it be progress if cancer were eliminated, or should that term be reserved for the elimination of its bases in the administered society itself?

Final Days

The end began in December 2021, around Christmas. She was still fighting. We had purchased a tree at our favorite nursery, the one that bestows names. Ours was a bushy spruce called Phyllis. Emanuela came with me, exhausted as she was. I remember looking over at her as she sat in one of the brightly colored metal chairs scattered around the place, waiting for me to load our pine: so tired, so fragile, so brave. In previous years, she would have carefully examined them. "Questo è un po' storto, e quell'altro è spennacchiato." (This one is a little bent, and the branches on the other one are like a plucked chicken.)

She would also never have passed up the opportunity to look around the shop with its seemingly random, but in reality highly curated, collection of little handmade items, limited-run books, and beautifully potted houseplants. The place appealed powerfully to her aesthetic sense as it had developed over those years of living in Berkeley: a mixture of craft and naturalism that was a perfect blend of the two worlds she knew the best.

Across the street was the yarn store where she had worked for several years—indeed, this corner of the world was very much hers. But I could see now that what she wanted more than anything else was to be at home. The months of chemo, the cancer itself, the constant worry about managing appointments, medications, and supplies—all of it had exhausted her. We had to go into the cancer center the next day. Emanuela was on her second clinical trial. It was something called an ERK inhibitor that was supposed to slow down, or perhaps block altogether, the vascularization of the tumors.

The relentlessly cheery interior of the cancer center, the brightly painted walls, the word "hope" written in a dozen languages and snippets of poetry here and there, was by now utterly familiar. The security guards who spent their days perfunctorily reciting COVID-19 symptom questionnaires to anxious patients—many of whom in truth were dying, like Emanuela was—recognized us on sight. They queried us in a quasi-apologetic tone that did nothing but alarm me.

When we had first come here, Emanuela would walk herself in. I was not allowed to come in at all because of pandemic restrictions; now, months later, I was pushing her in the transfer chair (lighter than a wheelchair and not self-propelled) that we had purchased, but which she had so resisted just weeks before. It was black with little colored butterflies embroidered on the back. I was somewhat proud of it. At least it was nicer than the horrible blue-and-gray things provided by the hospital. We made our way to the fourth floor. As always, she had her documents, her state-issued ID (she had never seen the need for a driver's license), her insurance card, and her COVID-19 vaccination card ready and organized. They were all together in a yellow-bordered IKEA sandwich baggie.

The wait began. A pattern had developed over the months that we had been coming. (Emanuela's note above describes it well.) After the check-in, I would often go back to the first floor to the coffee stand that had espresso and prepackaged Belgian waffles flavored with vanilla and something called "pearled sugar." Why did I have these things? The caffeine and the sweetness were somehow comforting; I would also buy Emanuela little gelled candies that she enjoyed.

The pursuit of these small vices was a way of mentally normalizing the visits, of making them seem part of a routine, like going to work or school. In that way, the situation could also appear to be stable: we were doing the same thing this time, as we had the last. But in reality, the situation was dynamic in one direction; the cancer grew: constantly, relentlessly, implacably.

Our physician's assistant (PA) that day had the last name of "Calabrese"; everyone, including herself, pronounced it "Calabreeze." Dr. Dhawan, the one running the clinical trial, was a young South Asian woman. Emanuela trusted neither of them. She had the sense that the clinical trial was a desperate bid that wouldn't work. Dhawan appeared on a computer monitor. The pandemic had reinforced the hierarchies among the medical staff: nurses and physician assistants were the only people to have any direct contact with patients, while doctors were disembodied images who read test results and communicated their meaning to patients through video chats. Indeed, in all the visits to the UCSF cancer center, Emanuela was never physically examined by a physician.

We sat in the blindingly white examination room, she on the thing that looked vaguely liked a dentist's chair, I on a plastic stool. The "numbers" seemed to be OK, except perhaps for her hemoglobin. But two worrying symptoms had now appeared, the terrible significance of which I did not grasp at the time: an elevated pulse, and slight hypoxia. Calabrese was also concerned that there might be some fluid accumulating in Emanuela's abdomen.

There seemed to be some disagreement, or at least a nonalignment of views, between the PA and the MD. "You might want to go to the ER just to check out what's going on down there," said Calabrese. Certainly nothing good could be going on "down there." Dr. Dhawan hesitated. Emanuela, who seemed to intuit that this was a turning point, asked if we could go to Alta Bates, in Berkeley. Calabrese assured us that she would "call ahead" and notify the ER of our arrival; this was all nonsense of course.

We would be at the back of the queue at one of the busiest intake facilities in the Bay Area right near Christmas.

Driving back from the cancer center across the bay, we were both in a quiet state of shock. The atmosphere was gray on gray, the I beams of the bridge recapitulating the steel-colored sky. When we arrived at Alta Bates, memories washed over me. I remembered her that morning, August 24, 2020, walking into the ER with her maroon pajama pants on, in pain but determined to get to the bottom of the problem.

I remembered her calling me on FaceTime while I waited in the parking lot due to COVID restrictions. "Amore," her terrified face said, "ho un cancro!" (Love, I have cancer!)

I remember later in the day, after she had been admitted to the hospital, walking with Eamon toward where I had parked the car and telling him that I didn't know how much longer Mom would be around, but also trying to assure him that I would always, always be there for him. His response, characteristic of Eamon, was to try to comfort me. "Mamma è forte" (Mom is strong), he said. Given the circumstances, this was an irrelevant truth.

All these memories of the recent past resurfaced as we pulled into the parking lot and I helped her into the transfer chair. It was cold. She, at least, was covered. But I had only a shirt, as I had expected to spend the day at UCSF, which, despite its open and light configuration, felt stuffy after a few hours. Of course, I was not allowed to accompany her into the waiting room. A new COVID spike had forced the hospital to again tighten its protocols. Thus, I left her there alone, with the man who was screaming about an imaginary metal plate in his head and the couple loudly arguing with an overwhelmed triage nurse. The only refuge was the lobby of a suite of medical offices across the street from the ER, which was unheated, but at least covered. I waited there.

After what must have been at least an hour, she was finally admitted. There was more shouting; several people were sleeping in the hallway on soiled-looking blankets. In the overly large room where they put Emanuela, there was a locker filled with donated clothes for people who either didn't have them, or whose were too dirty to wear. All of this, of course, was a rather normal scene for any ER; these institutions, in addition to trying to address the problem of critically ill people, function as holding pens and triage centers for the indigent and mentally ill in a society that offers no alternative to such populations.

More tests were done; her pulse was still elevated, her oxygen saturation low. They asked about her medications and did not know what to make of the clinical trial drugs. After an interminable wait, a young and energetic ER doctor finally came to talk to us. Following a brief and rather uninformative review of things we already knew, he finally came to the point. "Have you thought about hospice?" he asked. Shock washed over both of us.

"So soon?" Emanuela asked. That was, of course, the question. Hospice, after all, meant death. How was it possible that her life was ending so soon, when there was so much left for us. I had never shown her the Grand Canyon; we had not been able to go back to Hawaii to renew our vows; we had, more simply, not finished loving one another.

Then came the answer, in the form of a weird Marvel reference. "My spidey sense," he said, "tells me that's the direction this is headed." His "spidey sense," of course, would turn out to be infallible. But at the time we rejected it out of hand; or was it just me? She was, after all, still participating in the clinical trial, which must mean that there was some hope. "We are not ready for that," I said.

After he left, Emanuela turned to me and said, "Forse dob-biamo parlare di hospice." (Maybe we need to discuss hospice.) But we didn't really. Was this because of my self-delusion about what was happening, or was our denial mutual? Was this the moment when we were supposed to have a conversation about her "wishes," the one we never had? I have no idea; all I know is that we convinced ourselves, or at least I convinced myself, that we were still trying to fight the cancer.

She was finally admitted to a room in the hospital; it was a double that she shared with an enormous toad-like woman who listened to Fox News at high volume and alternately berated and praised the medical staff at the top of her lungs. By the end of Emanuela's three-day stay, we knew her views on her sister, and especially her sister's husband; we knew the menu for Christmas dinner at her house; we knew everything about the characteristics of her surgical wound and the disgusting drip bag full of blood and puss that she demanded be changed on a regular basis. We also knew about her culinary tastes. "This cottage cheese is dee-licious," "I've never had a sandwich this wonderful," and so on. But the toad, I had a feeling, would recover, while Emanuela would decline.

She was discharged, I believe, either on the twenty-third or on Christmas Eve. The floor doctor was a short athletic man with closely cropped hair and an air of busyness. He provided more grim assessments and raised again the possibility of hospice care, which we again waived off. He also prescribed medical oxygen. After some last-minute scrambling to secure the tanks, we made our way home. But now things were different. She could no longer sleep in bed; she had constant anxiety about breathing. A new symptom had also appeared during the ER stay: she had edema in her feet.

After this first trip to the emergency room, it was clear that there would be no more remotely normal existence for us. Emanuela's condition was fragile, and our situation at home was becoming increasingly chaotic. She needed constantly to be on oxygen, and I had constantly to massage her feet because they hurt. Our room rapidly filled with medical equipment and boxes as I now slept on the floor and she on the couch.

The cancer did its work. She was never comfortable. I tried to help, constantly arranging and rearranging pillows, moving her legs, massaging her back with camphor oil that came in a little bottle, called Kwan Loong, that our friend Nicole had given us. There was a spot on her lower right that seemed always to be a particular source of discomfort. And of course, there was the morphine (which came in little blue pills) and now the Ativan (which looked like aspirin) for anxiety and pain. Friends visited; Eamon spent more time away (thank God for Eamon's girlfriend, Romilly, and for our dear friends and neighbors Andrea, Nate, and Shu-Fan). Emanuela and I drew even closer; I think to a certain extent our bond shut out even Eamon, whom she wanted, up until the very end, to protect from what was happening.

Somehow Emanuela's obvious deterioration did not prevent us from getting back on the clinical trial. A phone call with Dr. Dhawan confirmed this. We were waiting in an endless line of cars at a golf course near San Leandro, the only place I had been able to find to get the COVID booster for Eamon and myself; Emanuela, we thought, was not eligible, although this turned out to be a misunderstanding. The three of us were together. Emanuela was looking out the window at the Canada geese standing impassively in the fields on either side of our car. For a time, I even asked Eamon to take the wheel so that I could adjust her oxygen. It was one of our last family outings, one of the last times the three of us were together going somewhere that was not a hospital. Dr. Dhawan called with the "good news." She had checked the protocols, and we could continue with the clinical trial. I felt irrationally giddy and hopeful. Perhaps the visit to Alta Bates had not been the turning point it so obviously seemed to be; perhaps, just this once, the ER doctor's "spidey sense" had failed him.

We returned to the cancer center, I believe on New Year's Eve. The bloodwork was, Calabrese assured us, within the trial parameters. But, I asked, was the treatment working? Well, said Calabrese, there was some evidence that the rate of growth of the tumors may have slowed. That did not seem to be particularly reassuring and, as it turned out, was, on closer inspection, wrong. But Calabrese's words left just sufficient ambiguity that hope, a sentiment that was now approaching self-delusion, could rush in to fill the void.

Time spent at the cancer center was at this point a strange relief for me. It was almost like going on vacation. I could leave for a few minutes, and the bed where she received her medicines was almost comfortable. The staff was polite and efficient, mostly; the room was clean; there was even a view of downtown San Francisco. I could relax a bit.

After her treatments this time, as we left the center, she had a strange request. "Andiamo a Napa; non voglio tornare a casa." (Let's go to Napa. I don't want to return home.) This was a complete reversal for Emanuela, for whom home was always safe; home was where our cat Pippo was, where Eamon was, where our books were, and her knitting projects. She was also never impulsive. Trips, even small ones, were carefully planned.

This reticence to return home, indeed the impulsive urgency not to go there, I now see was a sign that she was already leaving us—home was no longer home. She suddenly wanted to be anywhere but there. We picked up some clothes and Eamon, and headed north. I could see that our son was perturbed; his mother, the careful parent, the one who always made sure that we remembered our toothbrushes and had sufficient underwear, was suddenly erratic.

What did I feel then? "Distracted" would be the best description; the prospect of a little road trip I found somehow comforting. She would be in the front next to me; Eamon would be in the back. We could pretend just to be a small family on an outing, at least for an hour or so. Surely, I also irrationally thought, nothing can happen to her while she is in the car. It seemed like there was some sort of safety that must come from the little magical bubble created by the three of us together going somewhere.

Living with a dying person, especially a dying person with whom one is in love, is to experience a progressive foreshortening of time. *Next year might be terrible, but maybe we can have a good few months now. Next month might be awful, but let's focus on the week ahead. Tomorrow will likely be bad, but let's focus on today.* I was no longer thinking in these grand terms: months, weeks, or days. Rather, my horizon was defined by hours—minutes, really.

It was already dark by the time we left; we were still in the shortest days of the year. The drive went far too quickly for my taste. I wanted to stretch those forty-five minutes out as long as possible. John and Jessica welcomed us in. The house was light, and warm, and comfortable when we arrived, the opposite of the cluttered chaos that we had left behind. They looked worried. Emanuela lay on the couch. Her voice was beginning to fade, the result of the cancer having invaded her lungs; it pressed on her laryngeal nerve.

This was another way the cancer brought us closer together, for I had always to lean in close to her to understand what she was saying, and translate it for others if necessary. "Voglio solo tornare alla normalità." (I just want to get back to normality.) Such a simple, direct request, and also so totally unmeetable. "Anch'io," I said, "anch'io" (Me too). Did we stay for two days, or one? I'm unsure, but at one point we did venture out to buy a few things for her, and some shoes for Eamon at the outlet mall.

This totally banal excursion was a triumph of strength and will. She was exhausted, but still alert and engaged as I pushed her around the stores in the transfer chair with the embroidered butterflies. Eamon was bored and impatient—under normal circumstances, a completely healthy attitude to have.

At one point during the outing, I took Eamon aside. "I know this is tedious," I said, "but this may be the last time you go shopping with your mom, and do you realize the effort this is costing her?" I wasn't scolding him; I wanted him only not to regret anything, not to feel as if he had missed any moment that he wouldn't have back.

We returned to the house with the clothing, and I tried to make her comfortable. First, it was the TV room, arranging furniture and pillows; then it was briefly the couch; then it was the chair, the white upholstered one without arms. I slept for perhaps two or three hours that night. Her pulse continued to be elevated. The edema worsened.

I was standing in the kitchen—the same kitchen where, twenty years before, I had called her to tell her I was returning to Italy. Jessica and my father were talking among themselves in low tones. "She needs to go to the ER," said Jessica. "Her pulse is too high, and she has too much edema." My head spun; I tried to steady myself. The night before, I had vowed to both that I would never take Emanuela back there; the only result of our previous visit seemed to be a disastrous worsening of her condition: she had gone in without oxygen and without edema, and she had returned with both. I also knew the translation of what Jessica was saying: "She's dying."

After some discussion, I called Dr. Dhawan, and we decided to take her to the UCSF facility at Mount Parnassus: a massive hospital housed in a handsome building from the 1910s that sits atop a hill looking out across the city and the bay beyond.

One of the many puzzles our experience with the US health care system raised for me was the management of hospital admissions. Apparently, there is no bureaucratic way, or at least none that we had found, of directly accessing the hospital without going through the tortuous funnel of the always absurdly overburdened ER. The boredom, anxiety, and waste of this practice is indescribable. The same tests are run again. The details of the patient's history must be recited to yet another set of people; yes, metastatic colon cancer; no, she doesn't smoke or drink excessively or use illicit substances. Parnassus, however, was better organized, friendlier, and slightly more efficient than Alta Bates. Her information was also more legible since the computer systems they used were the same as those of the cancer center; these are both UCSF facilities. (That different groups of hospitals operate with different and incompatible charting software must be one of the unique absurdities of health care in the US.)

After a few hours of waiting, she was finally admitted. I could not come up with her immediately, as visiting hours, by that time, had ended and the hospital, again due to COVID protocols, was very strict about visitors. So I again left her, this time on a gurney looking frightened and disoriented, with her oxygen tank resting underneath the mattress. It felt like a betrayal.

I drove back to our house in Berkeley, across the bay. John and Jessica had driven Eamon home earlier, and he had eaten with our neighbors. I was exhausted and felt alone. From this point on, I would have to make a series of crucial decisions basically by myself. Emanuela was too tired, her moments of lucidity too few, and the questions of what the next steps were to be too pressing. I drank a beer, ate a bag of potato chips for dinner, and, after shifting the boxes and clothes strewn on our bed, collapsed on it.

For about a week, a new routine emerged. I would wake, get Eamon ready for school, try to get a little exercise, and then drive to Parnassus so that I could be there by ten, when visiting hours began. The visitors formed a long line stretching out from the hospital entrance; we were mostly anxious spouses, although most were full of hope in a way that I was not. My visits lasted the entire day, until eight thirty or sometimes nine, depending on the attitude of Emanuela's nurse that day, when they would finally kick me out. One night we watched *The Hunt for Red October*; it would be the last film we would see together.

Her room, in a funny way, was a little haven. It was on one of the higher floors, so the view was striking. In the evenings, a shell-pink sunlight would slip under the cloud line and pick out the city's buildings, throwing them into evidence against the steel backdrop of the sky. I had time to reflect, to wonder about the gray dawn that would come after this awful night. Furthermore, she had no roommate; no plaintive toad harassed her.

Doctors and specialists of various sorts came through: a fit and energetic physical therapist who exuded positivity, an occupational therapist with a mobile miniature golf kit, two late-middle-aged doctors who announced themselves as "palliative care specialists," that is to say, dispensers of opioids. The pair had a professorial air, wearing sweaters and blazers that contrasted sharply with the color-coded jumpsuits (green for specialists, blue for nurses, white for doctors) that everyone else wore. A "swallow specialist" came; he stuck a camera down her throat, with which he observed on a mobile screen whether the water from the green-tinted ice he had asked her to dissolve was leaking down her trachea.

A weird out-of-phaseness began to emerge between Emanuela's condition—she was quite obviously dying—and the small army of experts attending her, each narrowly focusing on a specific, and in the grand scheme of things not particularly relevant, aspect of her condition. The division of labor in medical care, doubtless necessary for many purposes, carries with it the danger of entrenching a blindness; for being in a state of dying is qualitatively different from having a "medical problem"; the recognition of it requires a totalizing gaze, an actual looking upon the patient, a knowledge of how she was before and how she is now. But every aspect of medical care seems to conspire against such a recomposition; it was as if the various dimensions of her health could be addressed in isolation from one another, as if they existed outside of who she was as an individual. Perhaps that is what the ER doctor at Alta Bates was trying to reference, this need for recomposition, when he talked about his "spidey sense."

(Scheduling brought home the absurdity of the situation most clearly. When we returned home from Parnassus, the hospital sent us a referral to another "swallow therapist"; they offered an appointment in late April. Emanuela laughed grimly at this. She knew already that she would be dead by then.)

At some point, the attending physician made the decision to discharge her. This was certainly not because her condition had improved, or even stabilized, in any real way. It was simply that they could do nothing for her, and they needed the bed. We crossed the street to visit the hospital pharmacy, where we picked up the pain medications, this time in oral suspension rather than in pill form.

Emanuela had now begun to make requests of me that were physically impossible to fulfill. (I would later learn after reading the, unfortunately quite accurate, brochure from the hospice service that this is an indicator of imminent mortality.) She wanted me to find us another place to live immediately so that she didn't have to return home; but of course, she also wanted me to be at the hospital during visiting hours. Indeed, she would grow impatient if I were not at her bed by ten and hated it when I had to leave. But, I pointed out, how could I even begin to find a place to live if I were spending, as I was, ten hours a day in the hospital? The point, again, was that she did not want to return home.

After collecting Emaneual's medications, we left the parking lot, an impressive ten-story structure built directly into the hill-side, but instead of heading east we went north again. Emanuela wanted shoes—ones that would fit her swollen feet. She thought a pair of Uggs would be the solution. She had seen somewhere that Nordstrom had them on sale, or was offering a wide variety of types, or something of the sort. (The red felted clogs that I had given her the previous Christmas with the word "love" written across them, and which she had so liked, no longer fit.) We crossed the Golden Gate Bridge and headed north to Corte Madera; the sky was flecked with clouds, highlighted in orangish-red by the setting sun—another one of those striking scenes that appear daily around the bay and that I had always vowed never to take for granted. It did nothing to lift our spirits.

When we arrived at the Nordstrom parking lot, she was too tired to exit the car and sent me instead to inspect the Uggs. I am not sure what I was expected to do; I think she had given me the size she wanted and I was to purchase a pair. I wandered into the department store in something of a daze: the cloying scent of perfume, the soft click of shoes walking on the fake-marble flooring, the indirect lighting, the attractive but overly made-up middle-aged women in pantsuits with golden name tags, and the fit and happy Marinites with coifed hair and tanned skin all seemed bizarrely normal. I had imagined, I guess, finding piles of tan, low-profile, comfortable-looking shoes in a wide variety of sizes. Instead, the Uggs on offer appeared themselves to have developed pretensions during their time in Marin. They had become flip-flops with fuzzy pink borders; some had turned into transparent plastic sandals, and others had even sprouted heels. The sizes, I discovered after a brief conversation with the shoe person, were all absurdly small. I returned to the car empty handed.

"Non ce l'hanno." (They don't have them.) Emanuela seemed already resigned to the news. Still, it was clear that she did not want to return home. She called her Italian friend Donatella as we pulled away from the store. They had met while Emanuela was working at the yarn store on Solano Avenue, probably in 2017. Just at the time Emanuela was diagnosed, our families had begun to form a close, indeed quasi-familial, relationship. Donatella and Emanuela had lived in the same neighborhood in Rome, their buildings mutually visible. By the time of the diagnosis, she was something between a *sorella maggiore* (a big sister) and a *zia* (aunt) to Emanuela: a sounding board, advice giver, and confidante on a range of issues for which she regarded my views as mostly irrelevant. She was also a link home. I remember her saying, soon after the discovery of cancer, "Ringrazio Dio per Donatella." (Thank God for Donatella.)

After a brief conversation, it was decided: we would go directly to their house to spend the night, and perhaps stay for a few days. When we arrived, Emanuela was weaker than ever; her pulse was elevated, and the edema had not improved. Donatella made her *brodo* (broth). She ate that night better than she had for at least a week. But Donatella took me aside in the kitchen. "Why did they discharge her?" I had no good answer. Clearly the hospital could do nothing for her, but it was also obvious that I couldn't take care of her adequately either.

I had to return home to talk to Eamon, who was puzzled and worried, and gather some things. Donatella drove, either my car or hers. "She's dying," she said. Over the next couple of days, Bob, her husband, and Donatella tried to convey this message gently but firmly. They knew that I had to face this reality, and somehow continue. Emanuela knew too. The first or second night at their house as I was trying to position her in the little brown easy chair where she slept, she leaned over me and said, "Dylan, ti devo dire una cosa." (I must tell you something.) "Che cosa?" (What?) I asked. "Voglio morire" (I want to die), she responded.

This was the beginning of the final phase. She was done with fighting; she was done with visits to the cancer center and with the drugs that made her sick; she was exhausted; it was over. "Cosa devo fare io?" (What must I do?) I asked her, fighting back my tears. "Mi devi lasciare andare." (You have to let me go.) "OK," I responded.

I wondered then if I had been more self-deluded than she, and for a longer time. Should I have encouraged her to think about hospice back when the ER doctor at Alta Bates had his "spidey sense" piqued? Was hope itself a kind of problem in our situation? The next few days are a blur. Bob and I visited a La-Z-Boy showroom where we purchased an automated recliner from a dubious-looking salesman who we both agreed had the air of a child molester. There was also a trip to IKEA to buy a rug and two lamps; a frantic clearing-out of the house also took place. Somehow, I ended up with a huge box of mint-scented fifty-gallon trash bags. I threw some things away. For some reason, her old tennis shoes, the purple ones, were one of hardest things to get rid of. I was in the yard surrounded by the detritus and chaos that seemed somehow to be an external manifestation of the cancer that was ravaging her body. Holding up the shoes that she had used for walking, *le scarpe da ginnastica* (tennis shoes), I looked at Bob, who was engaged in some project or other. "I guess she won't be using these anymore," I said. I knew where the wear on those shoes had come from: her favorite walk at Abbotts Lagoon in Point Reyes, her treks around the neighborhood or to Monterey Market, or to Solano Avenue. Her hikes through the redwoods in Mendocino, or in Tilden Park. All those memories were registered in the pattern of wear; her shoes were always consumed more on the outside edge because of the way she carried herself. They were molded to the movements of her body.

I understood then one of the reasons that Van Gogh was so obsessed with old shoes. No other item of clothing is so much a bearer of a person's particular charisma as their shoes. To say of a pair of shoes that they won't be needed anymore is to say that the person whose feet these shoes were specifically molded to through numberless walks has also somehow ceased to exist.

We got the house more or less arranged, and she returned home, but she was never comfortable again. Friends and family now rallied; Shu-Fan and Andrea came often. Evan and Sandra visited. Scott and his wife Katrina came. There was a constant stream of visitors; they were saying goodbye, I suppose. But then, there were the nights. Was it the cancer, or the morphine, or the

Ativan? In any case, a strange world emerged. One night we were surrounded by the Banda della Magliana, an organization of the Roman underworld from the seventies. Another time she grew angry because I refused to amputate her legs. She tried at one point to divorce me and move out. Lucidity always returned to some extent with daylight. But sleep was becoming scarce; one of our friends had given her a little bell, which she used to call us on account of her failing voice. Eamon grew to hate it, and he destroyed it after her death.

My family tried to help. Evan said I was bad at delegating, but I wasn't sure what to delegate and had no time to think about it. Caring for her was all consuming. At some point a commode appeared, which made the numerous nightly trips to the bathroom slightly easier to manage; but she still needed help with everything, always. Her decline constantly outpaced the health services available. First there was home health: a nurse to check in twice a week. The major contribution of this service was to provide us with a thickening agent so that she could take fluids with less danger of aspiration. It helped little and made everything disgusting. Then we transitioned to home hospice. They gave us morphine and Ativan in a "comfort package." I arranged for a hospital bed to be delivered. The La-Z-Boy was proving inadequate. Evan and Sandra left; the chaos intensified. The hospice nurse came; was this her second visit? The hospital bed was supposed to arrive that day or the next. I was completely exhausted. The nurse looked worried. She began to speak about "residential hospice" and something called "Bruns House," near Walnut Creek. I knew that this meant I was now in the business of deciding where Emanuela would die. As with so many other things in this experience, it seemed that the choice had been made by physical processes over which we had no control. I asked the nurse to contact the "Bruns House"; she became a fierce advocate and ally in this last bureaucratic struggle: I am profoundly grateful to her. She was wonderful and humane.

At one point, I was standing in the kitchen; the hospice nurse told me that I needed to speak with the staff to explain my situation. Jessica was there. I tried to be as direct and honest as I could. "I do not want the last memories of my wife to be of her in excruciating pain and suffering from hallucinations. There is no longer any way I can take care of her at home. Please help me." The directness seemed to work. She would be admitted that night. Toward the late afternoon, a transport vehicle came to pick her up. She was disoriented and frightened. They were young and inexperienced and had difficulty getting her down the steps. Then a comedy of errors ensued. I was following the vehicle, trying to maintain eye contact with Emanuela, who was looking out of the rear window. I could see her frightened face. The vehicle suddenly exited the freeway and turned back to our house. A phone call from the transport service, naturally a separate operation from the residential hospice facility itself, informed me that they had run out of oxygen and were returning to our house to see if they could "borrow some" of ours. The absurdity of the situation, a transport to a residential hospice facility that had insufficient oxygen, set me off. I became unreasonably angry with the two youthful drivers, whom I referred to as "a couple of fucking clowns," as I had to show them how to attach and use the oxygen tank. Jessica, again, had to witness all of this. I felt ashamed. But it was all so unnecessary; why, after all, was I not allowed to just drive her there? It would have been far safer, and less traumatic. We started out again and this time reached the Bruns House, an innocuous suburban ranch-style place in the shadow of Mount Diablo (a mountain that Eamon used to love, but which he can no longer look upon without sadness).

She was transported on the gurney through the back of the house into her room. I had to go through protocols and sign-in procedures at the front. Only one visitor was allowed at a time, but at least there were no limits on the visiting hours. Upon entry to the house, there was a nursing station to the right. Past that, along the corridor, there was a living area to the left with a TV, and some vaguely "spiritual"-seeming books; to the right was a large kitchen with a microwave and coffee machine. Her room was slightly farther down the corridor to the left.

The day she arrived, she was still lucid enough to be a presence in the world. I naively asked if it would be possible to take her out sometimes, on little trips around Walnut Creek, for example. They demurred. I was, of course, utterly self-deluded to think that she would ever leave that room again. She wanted me beside her; I helped her with her gown and asked the nurse to bring some ice chips, which satisfied her thirst to some extent without choking her. But the process of letting go had already begun; she was relaxing. The bed was comfortable. She had twenty-four-hour care from people who knew what they were doing.

There was a white board in the room on which was written "Welcome to the Bruns House" with a small heart drawn beside it. Under "goals for care," just one word appeared: "comfort."

Think of how all our future plans and hopes had imploded from just two years before. In the fall and winter of 2019 and very early 2020, the talk was of a trip to Armenia and Sicily, and perhaps a return to Hawaii; by the next year it was clinical trials and beating back the cancer long enough to prolong her life just a few more years; now everything was concentrated in that one modest aim, "comfort."

She slid away from life. On the morning of the second day, I headed back to Berkeley briefly to exercise and shower. The hospice doctor called me; we discussed Dilaudid, the powerful opioid. I returned to Bruns House in the early afternoon. She was sleeping. Eamon visited and was able to say, one last time, "Ti amo, mamma." (I love you, Mom.) I told her how much I loved her; I read. They had put a catheter in; she no longer needed me to help her to bathroom; I watched the basketball game off and on; the Warriors lost to Indiana. I had a conversation with one of the nurses. She was a devout Catholic from Ghana who had lost her sister recently to COVID. She wanted to know our story; I explained as best I could. That was perhaps when I first started composing this book.

She looked at me very kindly, and with something that appeared to be wisdom, and told me that I would be "OK," or something to that effect. I thanked her for the sentiment, but I also asked how on earth she could possibly know. I had not been "OK" for a very long time, and the woman that I loved lay suspended between life and death just a few feet away.

That night Eamon, John, Jessica and I ate at an In-N-Out; they dropped me off around six or so. I later went out to get a beer, which I snuck into the facility with the implicit approval of the nursing staff. I looked at Emanuela. Her face was drawn and waxy, and her mouth open. I walked to the nursing station and said that it seemed to me that Emanuela was "transitioning" (hospice speak for dying). After checking on her, the nursing staff assured me that she had at least a few more days.

I went to sleep that second night on the little foldout easy chair next to her bed. Around quarter to five the next morning, there was confusion, and I was awoken by a bustle of nurses surrounding Emanuela's bed. "She has a fever," one said, "104."

I got up to hold her hand. "She is still breathing, but won't take many more breaths now." I said to her, "Ti amo, amore; ti amerò sempre e non ti dimenticherò mai." (I love you, my love; I will always love you and I will never forget you.) A little cough, and she was gone. I looked around at the nurses, who were sobbing as they tried to comfort me. I wondered vaguely if hospice nurses were always so moved by the passing of their charges. I felt a crushing weight on my chest. *Dopo*, whatever it is that comes after, had begun.

Dopo

Passing. January 21, 2022

Dear All, This brief message is to let everyone know that Emanuela passed away today around 5:30am. I was with her, and she was peaceful. I will write more when I am composed enough to do so. Thanks again.

Loss. January 25, 2022

As promised, I'm writing a follow up note to my brief last message. It can have only one subject: loss. As Eamon and I try to move forward, we have constantly to deal with the gaping hole that Emanuela's absence leaves in the fabric of our existence. I have been aware that this has been coming for a long time. But it is no easier to deal with now that it is upon us. It shows up in a thousand ways: in dozens of half-finished projects of sweaters and socks that will never be completed, in plans for family trips that will never be taken, in Pippo's strange behavior now that the key member of the pack is no longer. More simply, perhaps it appears in the fact that the house itself seems gray and empty without her animating presence.

It is so hard that I find it necessary to spend large chunks of the day away and out, even as I try to declutter from the months of chaos that the cancer imposed on us. Acute grief comes in waves, between which a flat pseudo-normality ensues. It is as if some psychological mechanism prevents me from continuously facing what has actually happened. Denial and avoidance do have their uses. As always, you have all been enormously gracious and supportive. Many are asking me what they can do. The only honest answer that I can give you is that I have absolutely no idea. But as things become clearer and I can begin to figure out some order, I will call on your help.

Update. January 28, 2022

Today is exactly one week from her passing. I feel like I'm drift-ing, rudderless and without compass, on some enormous ocean of grief. What I had not realized is just how disorienting loss can be. For losing her, I have also lost myself as I was with her. Although I've not been terribly communicative for the last few days, rest assured that I know and feel the love and support from this community. Eamon and I are, in material terms, doing fine. We eat and sleep more or less normally. Eamon is engaged in school, auditions, friends, and so on. I do mundane things around the house and am starting to do a little work-related stuff again as well. In sum, I guess things are going as well as could be expected, as they say.

The Community. January 31, 2022

The richness and warmth of Emanuela's personality is mani-fested, as in a negative image, in the multifarious expressions of grief that her passing has provoked. We are mourning a teacher, a friend, a mother, a guide, a lover. Each one of us carries around a different aspect of this infinitely complex and beautiful human being. It will only be by coming together that we can truly cel-ebrate, even in a limited and partial manner, who she really was.

Stages. February 7, 2022

Grief is often thought of as a linear process; there are stages of grief (five of them: denial, anger, bargaining, depression, and acceptance). There is also the idea that time will heal; the loss appears, then, as an event occurring in a biographical timeline, which recedes gradually as life marches on. My sense is that it is not really like this. The stages, as most people who use this framework readily admit, can be experienced in various orders or, as I think is my case, all at once.

As for the notion of loss as an event, I find a different metaphor more useful. Emanuela's absence for me is like a gravitational force that determines the orbit of my daily routine. One might have the illusion of moving away, only to be sharply pulled back. Even the most mundane objects can set off a wave of associations that forces me again to face what has happened: a bank statement or coupon book addressed to her, for example. Or the little Post-it note that she left on the checkbook, "Inizia con questi!" (Start with these!) Her absence, in short, is a sort of presence that gives everything a specific shade and color. Grieving, I guess, is the name one gives to the process of trying to face that reality.

Rhythms. February 12, 2022

Grief has temporal patterns. Some are very obvious. For example, Valentine's Day is coming up: the first I've passed without her since 2000, when I had to attend a Fulbright meeting in Venice, which for some reason was scheduled on February 14. That day, she called me as I was crossing one of the numberless canals to tell me that her wallet had been stolen. When she went to the carabinieri to *fare la denuncia* (make a police report), they refused to accept it since Berlusconi had discovered an ingenious way to eliminate petty crime: by directing the police to no longer investigate or report small-scale street theft.

She was absolutely furious at the police, at Berlusconi, and at the Fulbright Commission, on whom she showered *picante* epithets (*teste di cazzo, stronzi, scemi*—dickheads, assholes, idiots) in roughly equal proportions. I felt fortunate to have escaped direct responsibility, but it was clear that we weren't going to spend any more February 14ths apart.

Other patterns are more subtle—for example, the fact that during the week, we were almost always together in the mid-morning, which makes this time of day particularly difficult for me; because that was when, with Eamon at school, we would make decisions together, discuss the news, or lay out plans for the future. For that reason, I am often out at that time, since Emanuela's absence becomes overwhelming.

Semiotics. February 15, 2022

One of the most poignant things about the experience of loss is the new relationship to everyday objects that it imposes on the griever. Yesterday I finished "A Grief Observed"; in it, C. S. Lewis describes the tendency to replace the real person with symbols, "a mere doll to be blubbered over." But there is another element to all of this: the conversion of everything into a symbol or a sign for her. I see the chair I bought for her in the vain hope that it might provide some comfort toward the end; the spindle that only she could animate, and which now sits idle; photographs, of course, everywhere, referring both to her and to a life that is irrevocably gone.

Many everyday objects to which I had previously never given much thought have suddenly been infused with a kind of sacred charisma. I spend hours contemplating a crocheted cactus pin-cushion because in some way it refers to her. But the sacred energy that invests all these little things also points up a painful chasm. For the signs are all I have; not the living, breathing person to which they all refer. The person and the icon of the person are not the same; attachment to the symbols, inevitable as it must be, is also a constant reminder of their total inadequacy. The signifier can never exhaust the signified, or even really approach it.

Event and Meaning. February 18, 2022

How should one understand the relationship between loss and grief? In one sense, the answer is obvious. I lost Emanuela, and therefore I am grieving her passing. (Or perhaps I'm grieving for myself. As Lewis points out, there is always the danger of a kind of narcissism of grief.) But the real connection between loss and grief is more complex and debatable. In what sense is the grief caused by the loss?

Many of the strongly prescriptive positions on grief see it as a reaction determined by the objective reality of the loss; therefore, grief can be divided into stages that are more or less universal, and that can be acted upon to speed along "recovery" (a term which strikes me as exceedingly odd in this context). But another position suggests instead that grief is quite underdetermined by loss; it can take instead a variety of different forms. In fact, loss imposes numerous choices on the griever concerning how to grieve.

The question of grief is precisely what to make of the loss, which is very far from being a straightforward matter; it imposes a heavy responsibility on the griever. One of the most important responsibilities for me is telling Emanuela's story: the story of her short, beautiful life. There is something redemptive about this process, because narration is a lending of meaning to events that perforce includes the meaning of her death. Biography, and indeed history as a whole, is a therapeutic for dealing with the tragedy of human existence. But do I have the strength and skill to tell her story, or at least some significant part of it? That is an open question.

One or Many? February 21, 2022

The loss imposes questions that one had confronted before as intellectual conundrums, but that have now become existential; they are no longer questions in general but questions for me. The one I am grappling with now is just this, "What exists? Many different things, or one big, interconnected thing?" I am no philosopher, and so I've undoubtedly formulated the problem in a crude and naive way. But Emanuela's passing poses it to me again and again.

The Buddhists teach that individuality (both in the sense of the existence of individual persons, and of individual objects) is an illusion that upon "reflection" (not quite the right term) is resolved by the realization of the interconnection among all things. The loss of individuals is, then, better understood as a fluctuation of the one big thing, rather than as absence. There is great wisdom in this insight.

But I must insist on individuality. I don't miss the state of the one big thing when Emanuela was alive; what I miss is everything that made her unique. I miss the way she sat, the way she talked; I miss her moles: the one on the tip of her nose that everyone saw, and the one on the back of her head that was well hidden by her thick and lovely hair. I miss the way she said my name (Dee-lan). Somehow, I have to acknowledge all this missing of particular things (there are an infinity of them that made up her). Perhaps the way through is to recognize that this missing of the particularities, that all this enormous pain that drags on day by day, is itself part of the one big thing.

On Being Awake. February 22, 2022

All good relationships induce a pleasant somnolence, which is a wonderful, warm gift. Routines and prefabricated decisions collectively constructed over years form so many cognitive short-cuts that organize and format what William James called the "blooming, buzzing confusion" of the world, and one's particular place in it.

This "operating system," if it is working well, allows for a certain kind of freedom and security. The loss of Emanuela is for me, among other things, like a system crash. Or, to pursue a different metaphor, it is like being rudely awoken from a pleasant dream. Much that was taken for granted becomes a question. This from the most banal things (what brand of shampoo, really, should I buy?), to more existential questions (whom am I exactly now?). The exhaustion of grief is in part a consequence of being so painfully awake all the time.

Senno di poi (Hindsight). February 24, 2022

Loss is learning. I think I told her I loved her every day that we were married; in fact, sometimes she would grow tired of it. "Mi dici qualcos'altro qualche volta?" (Could you sometimes say something else?), she would say. But although I knew that I loved her, I really did not know how much. Now, there is certainly no doubt.

One of the cruel tricks of human existence is that we really do not know what we have until it is gone; and then the knowledge of it seems a very poor substitute for the thing itself. Hegel captured the idea with his phrase about the owl of Minerva flying only at dusk, and so did William Bell with his beautiful song "You Don't

Miss Your Water." I don't think this is so much a matter of appreciating or not appreciating the present. It has to do with perspective, and thus is to a certain extent an inescapable dilemma. One can only appreciate the mountain from the plains, and one can only appreciate the plains from the mountain. Loss is the price we pay for knowledge of ourselves and those we most love.

Remains. May 23, 2022

There were two trips to the carpeted A-frame on Colusa Avenue. It was called Sunset View: appropriate enough, given its location. There was a gently running fountain in the front. The interior was somewhat dim and church-like, managing to convey an air of religiosity without displaying any explicit symbols of faith: crosses that weren't quite crosses, a Buddhist garden in the interior that wasn't really Buddhist, people dressed like priests who weren't. Sounds were muted and somber; the place was cool, as I suppose death is as well.

We were ushered into a small room off the main corridor. A tall, thin window let in some light; a couple of Monet-ish prints adorned the wood-paneled walls. Most of the room was occupied by a highly waxed oak table on which was mounted a plexiglass divider: a symbolic concession to the COVID-19 pandemic. I remember reading somewhere that such devices do virtually nothing to stop the virus, but perhaps the main point is to indicate a general air of responsibility.

A slightly heavy-set woman with shoulder-length brown hair and a pleasant face entered the room. After extending her condolences with well-practiced virtuosity, she handed me a yellowish sheet of card stock on which was printed, menu-like, a number of options. At the top of the list was a sort of all-inclusive one, pricing in at several thousand dollars. It offered a casket, a viewing ceremony, the provision of a religious figure who would look after such details as what would be said at the service, and of course flower arrangements. Even within this broad category of "full-service" funeral, several subtypes were on offer depending on such things as the quality of the casket, the length of the viewing, and the elaborateness of the flower display.

Below these items appeared cremation. One might think things would be simpler for this method, but the logic of differentiation was also powerfully at work here. Two main differences distinguished things in this domain: the type of container one would select for the cremation itself (cardboard box, pine box, full casket), and the receptacle for the ashes (plastic box, wooden box, wooden urn, elaborate ceramic urn). Failing to see what difference it could possibly make in what container Emanuela's body was cremated, I chose the cardboard box.

To select the receptacle, we followed the pleasant-faced woman to a room further down the hallway. Looking across, I glimpsed the casket showroom, ever so slightly reminiscent of a car dealership, with the makes and models set out in a carefully arranged pattern. Some were closed, but others were open, displaying their upholstered interiors. Was this supposed to give the impression that the corpse would be comfortable? In any case, our room was on the other side. It contained urns of varying shapes and sizes. They all resembled vases so that the feel was a bit like the pottery stores that Emanuela and I would sometimes visit when looking for pots for the tomato plants. I selected a simple wooden one—it is made of walnut and sits on my dresser.

(I remember thinking that the whole experience might constitute a rich field for some enterprising cultural sociologist of a particularly macabre cast of mind; she would show, presumably, how even in death the logic of class-determined consumption operated: middle-class people choosing the "sensible" middle-class urns, rather than the gaudy ceramic ones or the little plastic box. Perhaps the working-class families would be drawn to more decorative receptacles, and the upper classes something unattainable for either. Doubtless all of this would be shaped also by religious and ethno-national differences. *The Class of Death* would be the title: an instant hit opening new conceptual and empirical vistas.)

After having selected the urn, we returned to the room with the oak table. The pleasant-faced woman produced a legal-sized form that needed to be filled out in triplicate, indicating the numerous places I was to initial and sign. Yes, I was refusing my right to view the body; she would be cremated in a box, the ashes to be divided: one part in the wooden receptacle, the other in a black plastic box. I would, furthermore, be receiving two copies of the death certificate. (I was assured that they could print more, if needed, within one year; I wondered what happened after that.) The woman also intimated that the funeral home could assist me with the bureaucracy involved in legally transporting the ashes to Italy. She recounted that she had recently had dealings with the Italian consulate in San Francisco. "Those Italians like paperwork," she said. The final act was giving her my bank card, as if I were buying groceries, or perhaps an appliance.

It was at that point that the reality of the situation struck. I was deciding the details of how my beloved wife's body was to be incinerated. I was also made vividly aware that her body was in the place. Was it behind the desk at the front entrance, or was there another room off the corridor? And how many others were there with her? I signed the form and stumbled to the car, blinking in the sunlight.

We returned a week or so later. This time, instead of the pleasant-faced woman, there was a carefully groomed, unctuous young man with a red beard: more condolences and expressions of sorrow. I really couldn't hold him responsible for the obvious insincerity of it all; this was his job. But it put me very much off.

On this visit I noticed something else as well; there was a line of pictures on the wood-paneled wall documenting the founding and growth of the business. In the early years it appeared to have just been a cemetery. There were several pictures of a statue of an enormous stag overlooking the Golden Gate; it symbolized, I guessed, the "sunset view" that lent the place its name. At some point in the fifties or sixties, as horn-rimmed glasses and broad ties replaced the top hat and tails of the owner-founder, the A-frame had been built. Now it offered a combination of cemetery and "full-service" funeral parlor. A growth business if ever there was one, I thought grimly.

The unctuous man reappeared with two containers: a matte black-plastic box and the walnut urn. So that was what was left of her; no more flashing chocolate eyes, no more moles, no more beautiful hair, no more fiery temper, no more laughter, no more "Dee-lan." Just two dumb objects—one in theory to be returned to Italy, the other to stay with me at home, or to scatter? I didn't know; I still don't. We put them in the trunk and drove off. I now avoid that place as much as possible. It had been, when she was alive, located at an utterly unremarkable intersection. It was now the locus of memories almost too painful to bear.

Various. March 26, 2022

Yesterday, driving back from Sea Ranch (where my friends from the department generously rented an apartment for us), a flood of emotions washed over me. The beauty of the coast, which we had shared together so many times, felt cloying. A slight feeling of nausea rose in me. Was it all the twists and turns on Highway 1, or was it the vertigo induced by the fact that I will have to walk this earth without ever seeing her again? Both, I suppose.

Today I woke determined to "meet the demands of the day." I finally brought myself to water the garden, which I had neglected not out of slovenliness but because I couldn't bear to look at something that was so obviously hers. Now, however, it seems time to reengage, not so much because my grief is waning as because the living (Eamon, Pippo, the fish, the plants, friends, students, colleagues) have their rights and are not to be ignored. Above all, she would not have wanted me to cocoon myself; there is simply too much to do.

Office. March 3, 2022

Today has been a little easier, in part because I was in the office. There's a picture of her; we were in Cambridge just after 9/11. She's looking back at the camera, smiling and laughing. If only the picture were a portal; if only I could step through it and grab her hand and be whisked away from this gray-on-gray world where I am now. But after all, it's just a photo.

Statuses. March 4, 2022

Certain statuses, roles, and so on are socially recognized as containing their negation as part of what they are. The meaning of being a student is to no longer be a student. The meaning of being an assistant professor is to no longer be an assistant professor. But others are surrounded by the fiction of permanence. Among these of course are: "husband," "wife," "professor," or "adult."

Loss is, among other things, the stripping away of these social fictions. That's one reason why it's so traumatic to write "widowed" for the first time on a form; it marks one as being in the category of persons who have suffered the catastrophe of losing a status recognized socially as permanent. But the griever has a certain insight into the evanescence of all these statuses, and perhaps their "constructed" character, even the most generic ones, like "adult."

For "adulting" (the recent transformation from noun to verb strikes me as bearing a deep insight) itself is, of course, a collective project carried out in our society largely by couples. It requires a rather elaborate labor: decisions are internalized within the household, the flow of information is controlled, schedules are carefully coordinated. The status of being a "widower," or should I say the activity of "widowing," is quite different. It requires openness, sharing of information, vulnerability. In that sense one becomes, if I might put it this way, a "post-adult."

New Patterns. March 9, 2022

My relationship to my own grief is changing in a disconcerting way. Whereas before it was all consuming, now there are periods of the day that feel more or less normal. The grief must now be invited in, for example when I work on this memoir, or when I listen to music, especially to Verdi. Doubtless this would seem to be progress from the outside, but human consciousness, being that complex and devious mechanism that it is, lays other tricks and traps for the griever. For the lack of grief itself is a source of anxiety and feels almost like a second loss. When the tears return, it is strangely comforting; for more than anything the griever fears the loss of grief itself.

Happy Birthday. March 12, 2022

She would have turned fifty-two today; before 1950 this would have qualified her as elderly. Now it is simply "late middle age," a whole phase of life rendered possible for the vast majority of the population in the rich world by the techno-scientific breakthroughs of the post–World War II period.

I remember celebrating her fiftieth because it coincided so closely with the onset of the pandemic. I had spent some weeks before carefully planning the event. She was going to have a big party at César, the tapas place on Shattuck Avenue. The guests had been invited, and I think I had even begun to receive RSVPs. The situation, however, was turning ominous. By the first week of March, the vague and distant threat of the virus was becoming more concrete and local.

This was symbolized for us by the arrival of a cruise ship in Oakland that had to be quarantined. We could see it from the eastern span of the Bay Bridge. I had to cancel the event, which made me terribly sad because this was really the first time I had been able to organize something just for her. She was always celebrating others and seemed to have memorized everyone's birthday and thought about exactly the right gift for them months in advance. But I wanted this time, just for once, that she be the celebrated one, that she not have to worry about the details so that she could absorb the love that surrounded her.

It was not to be. I said to her, of course, that we would just organize another celebration when things "got back to normal." How was I to know that for us the pandemic would be the least of our catastrophes, and that normal was never to return? I made the best of things; we got takeout from César and I drove to San Francisco to get a Sacripantina sponge cake from the Pasticceria

Stella on Columbus Avenue and of course picked up a bottle of prosecco. We celebrated, just the three of us in our kitchen. That big birthday party has been permanently deferred, but I will always celebrate her. "Buon compleanno, amore mio! Ti porterò sempre nel mio cuore." (Happy birthday, my love. I will carry you forever in my heart.)

Artisan. March 20, 2022

Everyone knows that the first question that Americans ask one another at a gathering is "What do you do?" Which means of course, "What is your main source of income?" Implicitly, it is also a question about one's identity, which in that way is closely bound up in this country with the particular position a person occupies in the social division of labor. In Emanuela's case, this query would be hard to answer in a sense: she had numerous sources of income (teacher, yarn store employee, editor, translator, small-business person). At a deeper level there was a fundamental unity across all of these activities, and also those which are in our society marked as "domestic labor," such as cooking and childcare.

Emanuela was an artisan, by which I mean not a role but an orientation to the world. Everything she did, she did with extraordinary care: whether it was making lunch bags, or COVID masks, or hats, or tortellini, or preparing food platters for the concerts. Things were done well, and the doing well of things was an expression of love—love for her family, love for her friends, love for the community, and love of beauty. Among the infinite facets of her personality that I miss the most is this radically immanent orientation to work, this intimate refusal of the division of labor, with all its inhuman rigidifications and instrumentalizations over which we are forever stumbling in our imperfect attempts to connect with one another.

Memory. *March 25, 2022*

Today is my birthday, which prompts thoughts about time. We could think of the relationship of consciousness to memory like that of a train engine to its cars. Generally, the engine, and particularly the engineer sitting in her cabin, is oriented toward the future; at every station, however, the train picks up memories; but these are tacked on behind the other cars and are normally out of view. A loss like that of Emanuela, however, is a train wreck for consciousness; it throws the memories that are usually trailing in the background suddenly into one's field of vision.

Hence the dizzying sensation of simultaneity; buried recollections are violently brought forward. They may seem more real even than what happened in the very recent past. Time feels crushed in a vice, and consciousness, like an engineer thrown from the train and left to wander among the wreckage, surveys the detritus of its own past.

Language. *March 30, 2022*

One of the difficulties of writing our story is to decide what language to use. We violated all the rules one is supposed to follow in raising bilingual children. Italian was the tongue of our house, but we blended it with English, creating an almost private idiom. "Dobbiamo andare da Target a prendere uno swiffer." (We need to go to Target to get a swiffer.) "Ho voglia di un donut." (I want a donut.) "Facciamo pancakes stamattina." (Let's make pancakes this morning.) Sometimes Emanuela would spontaneously create new Italenglish verbs such as *checkare* (to check on, which should be *controllare* in Italian). At other times we would translate everything into Italian; for example, we called the Berkeley Bowl *la ciotola*, a translation of the shortened expression "the bowl," which Berkeleyians use to refer to the supermarket of that name. (It is, in any case, a bad translation since the "bowl" in Berkeley Bowl refers to the activity of bowling, not to the object.) When she watched the Warriors, she called the basketball player James Wiseman *l'uomo saggio* (literally, "wise man").

Italian, however, was the dominant language of our marriage, in the sense that it was the language in which we fell in love, and it was also the language in which we expressed our deepest feelings for one another. Among the infinity of things that cancer took from me when it carried her away is the ability to express these things to the woman I love and with the particular mood and feeling that only Italian conveys.

Quilting. April 3, 2022

As her husband, I have only my memories of her, an intense and brightly colored scrap of Emanuela's personality. At the memorial I had the privilege of seeing her through the eyes of her friends. They brought their own strips of cloth, each with a slightly different shade and color. The memorial itself was a kind of quilting set to music, the construction of a synthesis of deeply personal and subjective perspectives into some kind of image of who she was. It was not my memory alone, nor the memories of any of us as individuals; it was a collective memory, a product of the community in which her reality now consists. Thank you. It is a priceless gift you have given to Eamon and me.

Meetings. April 15, 2022

There have been many meetings; for instance, between our mutual friends and my friend Marco from Milan, with his new partner, Chiara. This provokes more reflections on time and the experience of it. My love for Emanuela was so all encompassing, our connection to one another so intimate and multifaceted that it broke certain relationships, like a magma dome splitting apart the stratigraphic layers above it. But in fact, these layers can be reconnected and, with her tragic passing taken up again, renewed and deepened. It must be emphasized that this is no "silver lining"; it is a brute fact, like her death itself.

Return. April 20, 2022

The city's character, its flat-topped Mediterranean pines cropped to look like enormous stalks of broccoli, the innumerable piazze that hide aesthetic wonders around every corner, the chaotic traffic and inattention to the requirements of pedestrian safety and comfort, and above all the light that lends everything a slightly salmon glow, very similar to, but somehow not as sharp and unrelenting as its Californian sister, is painfully familiar; here, unlike in Berkeley, the reminders are not confined to any specific object or place. The entire atmosphere exudes them. I am constantly on the edge of tears, but seeing Eamon pulls me back. He combines two qualities: the unbridled curiosity and wonder of the outsider, and the confidence and familiarity of the native who knows that this is his language, his family, his city. This gives me hope that something of us does, after all, remain.

Genitori (Parents). April 25, 2022

They have aged, as of course have I. Slightly more stooped, suffering perhaps under the twin burdens of having a daughter who could never grow up, and another cruelly destroyed in her prime. But they seem strikingly reconciled to their situation as well, focusing on Eamon, meals, practicalities. The mother appears at times eager to demonstrate her grief, contrasting her own distress with the seeming equanimity of her husband. But I believe none of it—neither the husband's apparent good cheer nor the wife's anguish. My sense is that they have not yet started to really grieve, that maybe they never will, and that perhaps in the end it is best that way. What good could come at this point from them "processing" their grief? Maybe the best strategy here is denial and avoidance.

Wandering. April 26, 2022

Eamon has ventured out across the city. We are slightly disconnected because he took my phone, the only one with service, although I note with some irritation that he seems not to have put his in "airplane mode." God knows what bill awaits us at home. I am a little concerned because this is the first time he has gone to the nonni alone, without my mediation and protection. Emanuela would doubtless have objected strenuously, but it seems right to me that he build direct relations with them. That, after all, is one of the points of this trip: to show to him that he has a rich network of familial and quasi-familial relations here. Sebastiano took us to lunch today, taking time off work to show us around the area near Piazza di Spagna; we ate at a very good sushi place. Romano and Eamon seem to get along well, and it seems right that he should be able to spend time with kids his own age. Alessia, after all, was her closest friend.

Here, I often feel at the same time both young and incredibly old. All my most vivid memories of Rome are when I was young and with her. Being here again, but now with both statuses reversed, throws into relief the specificity of my new condition: too old to be single, too young to be a widower.

We met Donatella's friends at the Libreria Borromini today. I asked the man at the cash register—who was white haired, with a slightly ruddy complexion and was smoking a cigarillo, emitting thereby the pungent odor of bookishness that one often finds in professors' offices and bookstores in Rome—to speak with Naomi. His face lit up as he called his daughter. She emerged on the staircase with jet-black hair and intelligent, sparkling eyes looking out from behind simple, stylish glasses. As soon as I explained who we were, "Siamo amici di Bob e Donatella" (We are friends of Bob and Donatella), her faced melted into a wide smile and introductions were made all around, including to the father, Paolo, the man at the *cassa* (cash register). She reminded me very slightly of Emanuela: her seriousness about books, her obvious intelligence. Not that they particularly resembled one another physically, nor that her social circumstances, superficially at least, seemed remotely the same. But both were bibliophiles and daughters of bibliophiles.

Delivery. September 10, 2022

We drove for a little over three days to reach the sprawling megalopolis on the Gulf of Mexico from our little coastal garden and college town. Over the course of the journey, Eamon became viscerally aware of the vastness of the country as never before.

The dry furnaces of the Colorado and Sonora deserts were followed by the red clay and white sands of New Mexico, where we saw at one point a sunset, a dust storm, and a thundershower simultaneously, in a single enormous panorama.

We crossed into the Lone Star State at El Paso. Eamon stared out the window, straining to understand this strange new place where he would begin a quasi-independent existence. Our hotel, a cavernous and seemingly almost-empty structure, was somewhere near the airport, and we were immediately struck by its gigantism. Instead of one room, there were two: one for sleeping, with two enormous beds, and another dominated by an indescribably ugly couch, which formed a sort of living room. Instead of a combined shower and bath, there was a massive oval tub and a separate walk-in unit. The building seemed designed to gratuitously waste space. A giant atrium with an indoor river and fountain was carved out of its center, separating the hotel into two wings. We wandered around slightly dazed by it all.

That evening we ate at a homestyle Mexican place, which was oddly positioned in the middle of an otherwise abandoned parking lot. Eamon wanted to speak in Italian, which confused the wait staff, who communicated with us in a mixture of English and Spanish. The general theme was abundance; the food was decent but mostly plentiful. The next day we headed toward San Antonio, crossing the brutally striking and unforgiving West Texas badlands. Who, or what, can live out here? An arid brown landscape littered with reddish rock and punctuated by the occasional mountain or mesa rushed by as we pushed on.

We stopped briefly to fill up the car in Van Horn (a Dutch name brought to the town by a US army major later imprisoned by the Confederacy, which was entirely inappropriate to the surroundings). As we were gassing up, a van pulled up alongside us filled with Korean Baptists from Houston wearing flip-flops, sunglasses, and ten-gallon hats: multiculturalism, Texas style. I tried to pay for the fuel with my debit card, but the screen was blank and unresponsive. Still, I was able to get the pump to work, but was unsure if I had paid. I thus had to enter the "general store," where Eamon was already inspecting the wares. This place was filled with an exotic assortment of geegaws: little cowboy-boot-shaped shot glasses, variously decorated cowboy hats, and "Indian" trinkets likely made in Asia. Eamon selected an "I love Texas" keychain for Romilly. The woman behind the cash register confirmed my purchase by producing a receipt while her colleague congratulated me on my honesty. "That's the kind we like around here," she said.

We pulled off. Eamon now began making sense of the place in the only way possible: through comparison, particularly with the Golden State. The rest areas, he observed, are much nicer in Texas; there are many more pickup trucks, and everything is bigger. But other things were disconcerting, such as the hap-hazardness of the street and highway configurations, as if the hostility to planning were so intense here that it had begun to erode basic infrastructure. The suburban buildings, too, seemed to express an even greater disdain for their surroundings than their, already awful enough, Californian counterparts.

Our second hotel, on the outskirts of San Antonio, well exemplified the genre. It was a giant polygon of indeterminate shape built around a central elevator; it faced the surrounding office parks and freeways (the term "neighborhood" has no applicability to such an area) with a blank brick exterior. On one side was a hideous and seemingly abandoned concrete courtyard dug into a sort of well. It was decorated with massive blocks that one might have imagined as the excrement of the main structure.

But the hotel's weirdest and most ingenious feature was the parking garage. This, instead of being in a separate location, was sandwiched between the lobby and the fifth floor so that the hotel proper was perched above it. (One advantage of this configuration that we appreciated only later was the layer of physical separation it created between the noisy graduation party on the ground level and our room.)

That night we ventured into downtown San Antonio with the idea of exploring the "river walk." We, or at least I, had imagined this as a sort of peaceful promenade through a public park. A worse description of the actual setup is hard to imagine. The "river walk" is physically quite pretty: a serpentine path running alongside a strip of grass with public sculpture scattered here and there. But the other elements made the whole thing seem like a cross between Disneyland and Las Vegas.

There were the boats that slid along the river itself, looking like giant pink, green, and yellow flip-flops, each packed with tourists listening more or less intently to a behatted guide going on about the various sights. At one point one of them picked out a man standing on a bridge spanning the river, with a camera poised to take a photograph. "Look at the Japanese guy about to take our picture," he exclaimed. "We all know how they are." The boat erupted in general hilarity. Eamon turned to me and grimaced; the sort of casual racism, at least toward certain groups, that would lead to banishment from polite society in California seemed tolerated here.

We also saw bronze statutes of Teddy Roosevelt and Davy Crockett as well as the Alamo: monuments to settler colonialism and white supremacy. The statues and the heavily African American and Latino throngs of tourists seemed mutually indifferent. The whole ambience was less elevated and more "populist" than it would have been in California.

On the morning of the fourth day, we headed toward Houston. Our surroundings greened and the air became thick. Eamon's curls tightened. We approached the city around eight thirty. Traffic was heavy, but not as awful as I had imagined. Rice University, our destination, is in the museum district: leafy green with low-lying houses and massive old oaks whose lower branches touch the ground and rise again, making them seem like huge wooden tentacles. We turned off the main street through a gate in the brick wall that sets the campus off from the surrounding neighborhood.

We heard screaming, cheering, and honking as the welcoming committee from Eamon's residential college greeted us. Sweaty late teens in shorts swimming through the humidity helped us quickly unload Eamon's belongings and whisked them up to his room. Eamon was drawn to them, his eagerness to begin the next chapter palpable and reassuring. I dropped him off and parked the car at the designated lot, about half a mile from the dorm. The welcoming committee had assured the parents there would be a shuttle to ferry us back to the dropoff point. I elected, somewhat foolishly perhaps, to walk. By the time I had returned to Eamon's room, my shirt was drenched with perspiration; half a mile in Houston's August heat is incomparable to half a mile anywhere in the Bay Area.

The dorm room was comfortable, spacious, clean, and above all air-conditioned. "Fine," I thought to myself, "he can live here." A lunch was served for parents and students. The former struggling to accept, the latter eagerly embracing, their new status. The poignancy of the official goodbye was heightened for us. I felt Emanuela's absence more than usual seeing the mothers and fathers anxiously imparting final scraps of wisdom; all I could say was "Pensa a Mamma" (Think of Mom), advice that was not advice, and was also superfluous.

I spent the rest of the day wandering around the area near campus and exploring the excellent and free modern art museums, made possible of course by the super-profits from fossil fuels, as was Eamon's scholarship. The Rothko Chapel was particularly striking: an interdenominational sacred space adorned with huge black canvases that people stared at while meditating more or less intentionally.

At the entrance was a collection of sacred books and a bound volume in which to leave dedications. I wrote to Emanuela, hoping as well that Eamon might come across it when and if he visited the place. After an excellent Vietnamese meal, I returned to the hotel to relax. Eamon and I saw each other again twice after the official farewell: once in the evening for ice cream sandwiches and then in the morning for coffee; I then left Rice Village and made my way to the massive George Bush International Airport. I returned to a "home" that can never really be one for me anymore. It is more like a shrine; Eamon's room remains untouched—the chaos of his departure still in evidence. The spirit of our little family pervades everything, the objective trace of a rich and busy life that exists no more. As work pulls me toward itself, or as I allow myself to be pulled toward it, I feel more and more like a visitor in my own house, which was once too small but has now become suddenly large and empty.

Difficult Nations. September 19, 2022

I have never been to Greece, where I have been invited for a talk, but at the level of the lifeworld, it feels completely familiar: numerous small markets, cafés, apothecaries, the occasional bookstore, chaotic traffic patterns with death-defying scooter riders weaving between buses and taxis. In one sense Athens seems an utterly generic southern European city.

Of course, there are differences, especially compared to Rome. The economic fragility is more palpable; for example, an elegant turn-of-the-century shopping gallery that reminds me of the big one in Central Milano, but completely abandoned, the windows still bearing the names of jewelry stores, upscale clothing stores, and restaurants that catered to people with incomes they now no longer have.

Then there is the empty shell of the Hotel Sans Rival, just down the street from where I am staying. Around the corner from the hotel stands an abandoned school, alongside which is a forlorn and garbage-filled basketball court populated by the stray cats that are ubiquitous in Athens. (Giorgos, my host from the Rosa Luxemburg Institute, misses no opportunity to pet them, which reminds me slightly of Emanuela.) The graffiti is also bolder and more colorful than in Rome, rising to cover most of the buildings from street level to three or four feet off the ground. But these are all differences of degree rather than kind.

A striking similarity between Rome and Athens concerns the way they exemplify the difficult relationship between their national and their ancient pasts. One of the things that drove Emanuela mad about the general run of tourists to Rome was how little interest they usually expressed in the country's national history. The throngs would rush past Il Museo del Risorgimento on their way to Trajan's Market or to the Forum. And how many paid any attention to the massive statue of Garibaldi that overlooks the Janiculum Hill above the Vatican? I have the same sense in Athens; in fact, it is more extreme. In the morning I visited the Museum of National History, located in the old parliament building. The exhibits, especially that on the second floor, commemorating the two hundredth anniversary of the outbreak of the Greek War of Independence, tell a story of the struggle of the "enslaved" Hellenes against their Ottoman oppressor.

There are certain oddities about the tale, such as the fact that no one seems to have been sure exactly what or where Greece was. One of the most important events, the attempt by Alexander Ypsilantis (the Greek Garibaldi) to raise an army of volunteers known to history as the Sacred Band, unfolded in Moldavia and Wallachia—current-day Romania. Furthermore, as the exhibit makes clear, the Greeks were scattered throughout the eastern Mediterranean in small, basically self-governing units. Did they imagine themselves to be a nation? In any case, the curators had clearly read their Benedict Anderson: a printing press was prominently displayed alongside the "traditional costumes" and other artifacts of Greek life before independence.* But the most striking thing about the place was that it was almost completely empty except for me and a middle-aged American couple: the three of us dutifully reading the plaques as we silently moved around the upper balcony.

The contrast with my early afternoon visit to the Acropolis was stark. When I finally reached the ticket office, it was approaching noon, and a lengthy cosmopolitan line stretched out before me. Snippets of French, Spanish, Italian, English, German, and

---

* *Imagined Communities* emphasizes the importance of printing to the rise of modern nationalism.

Russian floated above the throng, but there was very little Greek. As we tourists waited, the sun cooked us from above, and also from below as it bounced off the white marble paving stones that had been installed sometime in the sixties. In general, it was a good-natured queue: polite and relaxed families with couples young and old. I was the only single person, as far as I could see—a poignant reminder that I should have been doing this with Emanuela.

Affixed to the ticket office was a large white sign with the EU flag on it announcing that the Acropolis had been decreed a "European Heritage Site" and declaring, furthermore, that this was the place "where Europe began." Here, it stated, democracy, science, philosophy, and theater had been invented. Since apparently these pursuits and institutions were the defining features of "Europe," then it too must have been invented here. For a number of reasons, it's hard not to be skeptical of this massive dose of Euro-ideology.

First there's the problem of veracity. Is it really true, no matter how remarkable classical Athens was, that all of these things were invented on the Acropolis? Second, why was this the beginning of "Europe"? How can Europe, or even worse the EU, claim to be Athens's sole legitimate heir? After all, until the nineteenth century there was both a mosque and a church inside the Parthenon; Alexander spread Greek civilization far into Asia; and there is the obvious problem of North Africa and the significance of Aristotle for the Muslim world. Third, what of the current relationship between Europe and Greece? To call it strained would be a major understatement, given how much damage the Troika's ferocious belt-tightening measures have done. Indeed, it's no surprise that EU flags are very often defaced here.

Perhaps the deeper issue, which creates a certain commonality between Italy and Greece, is the difficulty of linking a prenational past of purportedly universal significance to a national present that seems to be a secondhand version of the more "advanced" West. Emanuela's irritation expressed precisely this issue. Both Italy and Greece face this problem: their greatness as civilizations preceded by centuries the coming of the nation-state, and the universalization of that political form relegated them to a "semi-peripheral" status. Thus the paradox of Italian or Greek national identity is that these nationalisms, while seeming to have an extremely strong symbolic basis in a charismatic past, can only access that past through the mediation of third parties who legitimate it as a common "European" one. The national population in both cases is thereby condemned to play the role of curator of a heritage that is not quite its own. One can understand, in this context, the hatred that the Futurists felt for the past combined with the fetishization of speed, the cult of the new, and the elevation of Milan to the status of an anti-Rome. Futurism was really an attempt to escape the trap of antiquity by establishing a tabula rasa on which to build a renewed national spirit. But this attempt, too, was also doomed to failure, since Futurism's cult of the new was compelled to refer to, and thereby carry within itself, the very antiquity it rejected.

Black Sheep. September 23, 2022

We must have walked four or five miles, wending our way first through the upscale shopping districts, and then passing by Syntagma Square, where the Communist Party was holding a protest against rising fuel prices, before finally strolling along the broad marble-paved walking path that skirts the southern edge of the Acropolis. The setting sun had painted the Parthenon pink. Giorgos pointed out the massive apartments whose broad windows and balconies opened onto views of the temple. Many stood oddly empty, a consequence of the fact that some of their politician-owners were languishing in jail on corruption charges. We took a selfie in front of the Hellenic Parliament, and as we continued our walk he gave me a brief history lesson. The main points he wanted to convey were these.

First, the Greek bourgeoisie was fundamentally diasporic. It had returned to "Greece" only after being expelled from the Ottoman lands as nationalism took hold. Second, Greece has historically lacked a class of large landholders. This was partly the result of the policy of its liberal national leadership to dis-tribute land in small plots so as to avoid the agrarian problem. Third, Greek urbanization had been extremely rapid in the 1960s. This had created a paradoxical cityscape: one that is at once very ancient and hypermodern, with little in between. The layering of historical levels one feels in London, Rome, or Paris is largely missing in Athens.

Our conversation wrapped up as we approached the "Black Sheep," the restaurant where we were to meet two of Giorgos's colleagues from the Rosa Luxemburg Institute, Rosa and Phoebe. Rosa appeared just as we settled down at our table. She and Giorgos embraced, and their connection appeared to embody an overlapping set of bonds that seemed almost familial; they were friends, colleagues, political comrades. Physically the two contrasted sharply: Giorgos was tall, dark, and slightly heavyset with an angular nose and intelligent brown eyes under a sharply defined brow; he appeared stereotypically "Greek." Rosa by contrast had bleach-blonde hair and soft features. She exuded energy, positivity, and fitness. The food arrived, along with the simple, refreshing wine that lubricated every evening I spent in Athens, and the conversation ranged widely: from Rosa's boxing classes and observations about how her fellow pugilists seemed to be searching for an outlet more fulfilling than either unemployment or their shitty jobs, to the legacy of the civil war of the late 1940s, to the American West and the foibles of US progressivism. Rosa described her upbringing as the daughter of a communist family in a deeply conservative village in northern Greece. The communist kids, she explained, played, ate, and socialized together, and above all did not go to church on Sundays. Her father traveled regularly to Bulgaria to meet comrades and perhaps to vacation; when he returned to Greece he would try to point out that not everything was going well up north. Given this background, it was no accident that she shared a name with the institute. Phoebe also described her political formation, explaining that she had worked in some capacity for a UN agency in Berlin but had grown disillusioned with their do-nothingism and was now back in Athens, excited to be involved in the institute.

Toward the end of the evening, I posed a question to the group. "Could any of you ever imagine being romantically involved with someone not on the left?" They laughed, a bit taken aback by my query. All of them, after a brief consideration, rejected the idea. "It might be exciting at first," said Rosa, "but to be on the left is to adopt a view of the world, a way of life." The others agreed. This, of course, points to an important difference between the US and those countries that have had substantial communist or at least Marxist movements and parties. In Greece, or Italy or France, political traditions are rooted in a social milieu that spreads out from the sphere of formal politics and toward leisure time, friendship, and romantic attachment. In the US, by contrast, the spheres of politics and everyday life remain sharply distinct.

To restrict one's friends or circle of potential partners to "the left" would mean either social isolation or membership in a cult or sect. It is possible that this is changing to some extent now, as the widely condemned but in my opinion quite healthy and normal phenomenon of "political polarization" would seem to show.

But caution should be used here, as the specificity of the US often disables comparisons and apparent convergences. For the American version of political polarization cannot be understood in terms of the historical categories of left and right as they emerged in Europe after the French Revolution. One might restrict oneself exclusively to Democratic Party voters in social interaction for decades without ever meeting a person of the left. This is true even within the Sanders wing of the party, which encompasses an amorphous spectrum of opinion stretching from Brandeis-type partisans of the regulatory state to the varieties of Kautskyist who shelter under the banner of the Democratic Socialists of America. The lack of a tradition, or a shared set of intellectual references, or a worldview in the strong sense will take decades to repair. In the meantime, to be on the left but also to be a person in the US demands a sort of lived eclecticism or an embodied pluralism that is quite distinct from the experience described by my Greek hosts.

Fritz. September 23, 2022

The Rosa Luxemburg Institute is an admirably international-ist organization, with branches in several European countries as well as in the US and Mexico. But it is an internationalism with "German characteristics." This is particularly evident in the leadership of the local offices. Each branch must have a German director; in the Athens office, his name is Fritz. The evening of the presentation, he stood out immediately as an exemplar of his national type among the Greeks; he had close-cropped white hair, a triangular nose, an earring, and was wearing a pink linen shirt that seemed a bit like beach clothing. I was most struck by his sad gray eyes. His manner was ever so slightly formal and obsequious, something I had not experienced from any of the Greeks. But he later revealed himself to be a profoundly sensitive and perceptive soul.

We were seated across from one another at the lovely taverna where the institute had organized a post-seminar dinner, and he explained the difficulties of his situation. Above all there was the matter of the language. Fritz was taking classes, but it was slow going, and the Greek alphabet added another layer of difficulty. He felt isolated, and missed Berlin. At dinner he was the only person to order a beer; I had briefly considered asking for one, too, in order to soften his sense of isolation, but elected at the last moment to drink wine because it went so well with the food. As I did so, I felt slightly guilty, as if I had somehow betrayed him. He then asked if I had a family.

This was the first time the question had arisen in this sort of setting since Emanuela's passing, and it recalled the numerous times I had spoken of her and described our lives together to relative strangers after giving a paper or speaking. I found myself saying in reply that I had once had a family, but that my wife had died tragically and that my son now attends college in Texas. Poor Fritz clearly felt that he had committed a tremendous faux pas by asking me, but it was quite natural for him to do so since I was still wearing my wedding ring. In fact Fritz's question had been prompted by an observation that showed him, at least in my view, to be a remarkably observant person. He said that he had noticed during the question-and-answer session that I was touching my ring as if to draw comfort from it. I was not aware of this, but was grateful to him for having pointed it out. It made me feel somehow near to her. I then asked if he had ever been married. "Once, for five years," he replied. "We parted amicably, and I realized that I'm just not meant for that sort of thing; better to be alone." Somehow this made his sensitivity even more evident.

At this point, a fascinating episode started to unfold. It began with Rosa, who, as I was coming to understand, wielded an easy charismatic authority in dinner conversation, turning the discussion toward a mysterious episode in her father's past involving a deployment to Cyprus in the sixties. Fritz seized the occasion opened by Rosa's story to share a rather extraordinary piece of his own family's history. He had been going through his grandfather's papers and had found a letter—it must have been from the late 1930s—written by the local party official warmly recommending his grandfather for a position as a veterinarian. The letter deplored the local situation, where nonparty individuals were advancing in their careers while old Nazi Party members such as Fritz's grandfather could not progress. The situation was all the more scandalous since the grandfather had been involved in an important paramilitary action as a member of the SA (the earlier, more plebeian version of the political police before the rise of the SS) in 1932 that had resulted in the death of a communist. Fritz had become obsessed with researching the incident, so as to better understand his grandfather's part in it. This led him to the discovery of a large archival box containing a photograph that, to Fritz's astonishment, showed his grandfather not only participating in the incident but leading a column of SA men through the town where it had taken place.

He then pulled out his cell phone and showed us a picture of the column with an imposing bald man at its head who, he said, was his grandfather. "What became of him?" Rosa asked. To which Fritz replied, "Stalingrad." We all expressed some skepticism about that, as he was clearly already well into middle age in 1932 and must have been in his fifties by the winter of 1941. But Fritz reminded us that he was a veterinarian, and such persons were highly valued in the Wehrmacht because of the importance of horses to Hitler's armies. "Family history is fascinating," commented Rosa. "There is always a dark secret to be revealed." "Especially among you Europeans," I joked. To which she quite rightly responded that there were certainly dark secrets in American family histories too. True enough, I thought to myself, although the American twentieth century had been so comparatively placid that its population has been somewhat insulated from those fundamental political choices that many Europeans have had to face, and which generate, after all, the dark secrets to which Rosa referred.

Houston. December 2, 2022

Now that I am traveling more, to visit Eamon, several important changes are evident. It is obvious that Uber, or more generally "app-based rideshares," are no longer just an option; they are a necessity. Furthermore, Airbnb has radically transformed the market for temporary shelter. These changes have been devastating; the first has undermined the conditions of existence for taxi drivers everywhere, and the second has gobbled up housing stock like some toxic algal bloom, creating dead zones in the center of every major city on the globe.

Upon arrival in Houston, my plan was to use Uber to reach my Airbnb; I felt rather smug about the whole thing. How fluent I was becoming in the use of my phone! The signs for ground transportation in Houston reflected the new reality, showing the degree to which the Texan metropolis had moved more rapidly into the future than San Francisco. At George Bush International the sign for "Taxis" has been decaled over with "App-Based Ride Services," indicating the place where at one time there would have been a dispatch queue. As I emerged from the airport, the physical remnants of that bygone age were evident: an old booth, and a snaking traffic pattern that not so long ago would have been full of brightly colored vehicles clearly marked out as taxis. At the time, a queue overseen by an impartial, if harried person, the dispatcher, a guarantor of basic fairness and order, also would have been evident. In place of all this there was now a random collection of cars driven by a class of more or less super-exploited neo-peasants, perhaps laboring under the misconception that they actually owned the means of production, when in fact all they possessed was the right to pay the depreciation costs of their vehicles out of their own pockets; they picked up cell-phone-glued passengers scattered about haphazardly, singly or in small groups, in no apparent order. I put in my destination and location and waited.

After a few minutes I was "matched" with a driver whose icon I could see moving slowly toward me on my screen. Then a disconcerting notification, "Your ride is no longer available." I tried again; I repeated the same process three or four times before "Sharif" finally agreed to take me from the airport. As his car pulled up, a nondescript red Toyota Camry, I greeted him as a savior. "Thanks so much for picking me up. You're out late." It was well after one by this time.

Sharif turned out to be an enthusiastic booster for his hometown. There were three reasons, he said, that he loved Houston: its diversity, its food, and its large stock of affordable housing. As we sped along the massive highway network through a seemingly endless suburban sprawl in which Whataburgers, gun stores, and storage facilities rolled by as if we were driving alongside a giant mural of repeating images, it began to rain. I was slightly anxious. Would the "Latch" app, which I'd downloaded to access the key codes, actually work? By the time Sharif dropped me in front of the gated apartment complex where my Airbnb was supposedly located, water was cascading out of the sky. Naturally I had no umbrella.

I exited the car with my belongings and took shelter under the eaves of the complex's front office, which was firmly locked. My phone's screen was splattered with water droplets, and it took several minutes of fumbling simply to open the app. I managed to locate the two numbers: one for the "central door" and the other for the apartment. I began to look about for a place to enter them but found nothing. A small pedestrian gate to the left of the main door had a keypad, but the numbers only went up to five, whereas my code made use of the entire range. The situation seemed hopeless. I was on the outside of the apartment complex in the pouring rain at nearly two in the morning with a useless series of numbers.

Luckily, just at that moment, a vehicle arrived and the large gate for cars slowly creaked open. Seizing the opportunity, I slipped through behind the car, before the gate closed. I was now on the bottom level of the building's massive parking garage. I worked my way through a labyrinth of steel and concrete passages seemingly designed to prevent any pedestrian access, until I finally found my apartment: 1225. But another problem now cropped up. How would I enter the numbers?

Above the door's lock was a flat black disk that seemed to have something do with "Latch" but on which no numbers were visible. We stared at one another. As I fumbled around with the handle I accidentally brushed against the plate and for a brief moment a ring of glowing digits appeared around the circumference. Relieved, I entered the numbers. The door miraculously unlatched and swung inward, revealing a sterile apartment decorated with prefabricated "witty" statements painted on little gray wooden placards. The one in the kitchen read, "I cook with wine, sometimes I even put it in the food." I surveyed my surroundings, brushed my teeth, and collapsed on top of my bed's hideous yellow floral duvet cover.

I woke early the next morning, had my coffee, and walked toward the Rice University campus, crossing the nondescript expanse of Hermann Park flanking Bay's Bayou, a slow-moving river channeled by a giant concrete bed. When I reached the campus, I was struck again by its beauty. Lining the main avenues were massive live oaks covered with air plants, identical to the ones sold at astronomical prices in fancy little gift and flower stores in the Bay Area, and which from a distance are so thick they look like Spanish moss. Interesting buildings and striking sculptures could almost make one forget the campus's "Youngkin Center" and the sordid details of William Marsh Rice's death in 1900, when he was evidently murdered by his valet, who was enslaved, as part of some plot to gain control of his estate. I had arrived somewhat early and waited in front of Eamon's dorm.

He appeared after about ten minutes, wearing the gray leopard-print sweater he had purchased on his trip to England last summer. We embraced; it felt good to see him again; he reminded me so much of his mother: all long hair and chocolate eyes and kindness. He took me to his favorite place to eat breakfast, a charmingly slow and chaotic espresso bar run by students and full, at that hour, of bleary-eyed faculty members (it was really too early for the college students) dosing themselves with caffeine and putting the final touches on their lectures.

The next couple of days were a bit of a blur. I settled into a routine of working in the library while Eamon was at class. I met his friend Sam, who had lost his father, a famous conductor and a presiding spirit of the Shepherd School (the music school housed at Rice). I was able to attend three performances: a commemorative concert for Sam's dad, Larry Rachleff; Eamon's solo cello recital, at which he played Respighi; and an orchestra concert. Seeing Eamon play, especially at the recital, was more poignant than I realized it would be. It was not the first concert of his I had attended since Emanuela's passing, but I felt her absence as a crushing fact. It seemed so terribly unjust that she, who had given so much so that her son might be here, was not. Eamon, too, was thinking of her, always of course, but especially in these moments.

The night after the orchestra concert, we ate with the mother of Eamon's roommate Alejandro, his two brothers, and his sister. They were from a small town outside of Houston; the mom, Diana, seemed illuminated from within by positive energy and overflowing with pride and love for her children. We ate from food trucks parked in the area: a Korean hotdog place and a taco stand. It was definitely undergraduate food: tasty, cheap, calorific. Diana and I exchanged complaints about the implications of such a meal for our late-middle-aged bodies. The next morning Eamon and I breakfasted on crêpes: oddly, there are two places serving them within a couple of blocks of one another in Rice Village. After we finished our sweet and pleasant meal and I had, as usual, tried to offer some rather irrelevant advice (it is impossible, I think, after so many years of being a "dad" not to do that), I expertly hailed, if that is the correct verb, an Uber. If the trip had taught me nothing else, it had at least reconciled me to the ineluctable condition of device servitude: *technoféodalisme* indeed.

Fireside. November 24, 2022

The assorted crew of opaque theorists who talk about the death of the subject and raise questions such as "Who is the author?" do, after all, have a point. I grasped it by the guts when Emanuela's death shattered my own, as it turned out, quite tenuously knitted-together "identity." Her presence gave everything a definite narrative shape. There were memories, and then there was the now, and whatever was to come. Even when I connected with friends I had known before, it was from a definite perspective: that of the unified and unifying present. This time differed.

When I returned to Louisville to visit my ailing mom, Amy, whom I had not seen since Los Angeles, had invited us over. For various reasons, family obligations, and the general tiredness that plagues late-middle-age existence, only Matt, with whom we had traveled across the country long ago, and I were able to come. The plan was to sit around a firepit. I was skeptical. Louisville is not an especially cold place, but it certainly has winter, and the idea of sitting in a backyard in late November, even with blazing logs, made me shiver. But I wanted very much to see them both, so I zipped up my absurdly thin Uniqlo jacket and pulled down the orange hat with carrots on it that Eva had lent me and told Eamon I would be back in a couple of hours. "Have fun, Dad," he said. I felt vaguely like a guilty teenager.

Amy had rented an Airbnb near Frankfort Avenue, a very pretty neighborhood, most of which must have been built in the twenties and thirties. Reaching the house required driving up a brick-paved street: South Peterson. As a teenager I must have done that hundreds of times, first with my mom, and then when I got my license by myself, on my way to violin lessons at the "academy." Bumping up it this evening in the tiny Honda Fit owned by my mother, Peg, raised again the perennial question: Why had this one half street, out of the whole city, been left with brick, so that passengers and drivers would rattle around like dice in a box as they climbed the hill? Was an overly zealous neighborhood association responsible? Perhaps they had always been there, but I had noticed on this trip back the numerous flags proclaiming more or less dubious local identities. For example, I was surprised learn that I had grown up in the "Douglass Highlands," according to one such banner. Maybe a small group of civically minded fanatics defended the bricks against all comers as a sign of the distinctiveness of their little patch. I turned off Peterson and wended my way back toward a dead-end street on a hill called Saunders. Toward the end on the right, as I descended, was the little shotgun house that Amy had rented.

Matt arrived at exactly the same moment. He was driving a large white truck; it was an upgrade from the vehicles I had remembered him in. When I had been in high school, and he just out, we tooled around in a tiny stick-shift Toyota. We embraced, but he cautioned me not to touch his shoulder, which had suffered multiple tissue tears from overuse in cooking. He had a selection of firewood in the truck bed: some slightly rotten-seeming wedge-shaped logs, some leftovers from a carpentry project, and various branches and twigs for kindling. We were both older, of course: wrinkles here and there, bits of gray hair, faces careworn. But he was still Matt: all energy and positivity and plans, with two bottles of very good-looking wine, together with the wood. I had shown up empty handed and felt slightly foolish about it. In part this had been intentional, because I wanted to avoid a multiple-bottle evening. But I could have at least provided olives or crackers. Family activities, visiting Peg mostly, had eaten up the day.

Amy appeared at the door of the house, warm and natural as ever. We embraced, and then the three of us walked through the newly painted and tasteful but exceedingly simple shotgun. I made some overly enthusiastic remark about the refrigerator, perhaps as a way of smoothing the interaction; but as we exited the back of the house and came upon the firepit, the conversation became more natural.

Somehow we each fell into our appointed roles; as the wine loosened our tongues, we reminisced about that trip to San Francisco thirty years before: Amy's inability to reach the pedals without crushing us all forward on the single bench seat in the front of Matt's cab, gas money in an envelope, shopping for jewelry for Susan, whom Matt would later marry, at the various Navajo trading posts that we came upon in New Mexico and Arizona. (All this stuff had been stolen out of Matt's truck on a trip to Manhattan some years later.) "Why," I thought, "hadn't it occurred to me to buy something for Amy on that trip?" Presumably, I had no money. It was, in any case, a taking up of threads that had been dropped decades before.

The experience was disconcerting because in reminiscing, I felt I was again that person, the one I thought long dead, or so submerged in my subsequent accreted selves as to be undiscoverable by me, whoever that might be. (For example, I tried to protect Amy from melting her shoes, but failed to do so, which somehow reminded me of us as teenagers. Matt then told us a story about how Jon, another friend of ours, had burned his shoes entirely on some debauched camping trip decades before, at which we all laughed.) Perhaps the reason the immediacy of this reconnection was so disconcerting is that we tend to think of our accumulated experiences, and thereby our personalities, like a complex and well-made stew. In this model, the earlier selves are well assimilated to the latter and stand in a relationship of base or roux to the finished product. But I think it's probably better to think of personalities as more like layer cakes. The levels are somehow held together, but they maintain their integrity so that they can be accessed instantly through recollection or trauma or being together again: processes that cut through the cake like a sharp knife, thereby revealing the layers. Which poses the unanswerable question: Which of the layers am I, and if all of them, then in what relationship do they really stand to one another?

Health Care Summary. May 2, 2022

They come printed on white paper in multicolored ink. The header is a picture of cyclists, a man and a woman, looking over an ocean: the Pacific perhaps? They are supposed to be the image of late-middle-age vigor and health. Doubtless they regularly check their MyHealth portals and have six-month checkups. Below the header sits a blue-bordered rectangle listing "helpful resources," a chat service called "Sydney Health" and a phone number. Further down, two smaller green rectangles are arranged side by side: "claims summary" and "preventive care reminders." Under the care reminders, four words appear: "For Emanuela, Flu Shot"; I'm unsure what is more striking, their phony solicitousness or their cruel absurdity. The claims summary is weirder still; it contains four items: "Doctors/ Facility Charges, $14,787.47"; "Your Discounts, 11,076.65"; "Due to Your Doctor/Facility, $3,710.82"; "Anthem Blue Cross Paid, $3,690.82." Thus, the copay is $20.

One wonders what this all means. Was there ever really a "service" (helping Emanuela to die, for example) that cost over $14,000? Or rather should the "charges" be regarded as the opening bid in what is basically a political struggle between doctors and "facilities" and the insurance company, who in this case imposed a "discount" of 75 percent? And why, more importantly, am I being presented with this information? Is it supposed to be a gesture toward "transparency"? If so, it fails entirely. I have no idea what medical service is even being discussed, and the charges and discounts raise far more questions than they answer. In general, of course, this is just one of many examples; Emanuela is gone, but her bureaucratic trace remains in a thousand computers linked to insurance companies, credit cards, mail-order catalogues, and marketing departments that mindlessly churn out paper targeted to a customer/patient/consumer who no longer exists; receiving them is just another little torture for the bereaved, concocted by an administered society for which death is invisible. One could escape it, presumably, by contacting all the various spewers forth of junk mail; but in this case the treatment, as they say, really might be worse than the disease.

The Durability of Disposable Things. July 28, 2022

It seems somehow wrong that the duration of banal everyday items, soaps or cleaning supplies or foods, for example, should extend beyond the life of those we love. We purchased a large bottle of shampoo together, probably a month before she died. I had asked myself at the time if she would survive until we had used it up. "Of course," I thought. Such items don't outlast their purchasers. They have to be replaced. This feeling is so strong that the objects can become a kind of talisman seeming to guard against death.

Such superstitions derive from our normal relationship to everyday items of consumption, since their disposability typically describes their evanescence, at least as use values if not as waste, in relation to our own lives, which thereby gain the appearance of eternity. But disposables lose their disposability if the life of the consumer is foreshortened so that the object's duration extends beyond that of hers. Then it becomes something else: the bearer of memories, a reference pointing back to the time when she was there. There is some line on the shampoo bottle that indicates the volume of liquid it contained the day she died, which sacralizes it.

Time's Passage. August 9, 2022

The recognition is slowly dawning that she is in the past. It seems obscene somehow, but looking back at the photos and the videos, the signs of time's passage are everywhere: in the way that she looked, of course, before her hair acquired its streaks of gray, and how Eamon was, a dynamo of unrestrained positivity before the emotional tempest of adolescence, before he had to deal with falling in love, and of course before his mom fell ill, when she could still seem an eternal presence, *la mia roccia* (my rock), as he called her, an absolute reference point both to push against and to be linked to, or to be linked to precisely in pushing against.

There are also little features of the lifeworld that already show that now is somehow a slightly different period than then. The cell phones and iPads that appear in the photos are clunkier; the adaptors subtly differ. There are the slight changes in the house: the new configuration of the shelves, for example; the books that are not quite so numerous.

All this serves to point out that the opening of the present is no longer the now of her; it is not even the now of her passing, which was its own highly distinctive period. I wouldn't want to say, of course, that I have lost my relationship to her, since in an important sense that connection is internal and constitutes a crucial part of who I am. But the dialogue has become a monologue, or a dialogue with her memory, which is precisely my memory of her, hence an internal rumination. It is hard to resist posing questions such as "What would she think of what I am doing?"; "Would she approve?"; "Is my acting in this way a betrayal of her?" But perhaps a better way of "living in the light of" is to try to hold on to the skills that she taught me, rather than to enthrone her memory as a kind of moral authority.

For better or for worse, I have to make, and assume responsibility for, my own decisions now. But I can at least do this thinking about how she would have evaluated things, how the information would have appeared to her. This requires that I see the world through her eyes, or from her perspective; and that, in turn, requires the skills of a novelist, not a sociologist. Hence, the connection between her passing and my faltering attempts to create for myself a new style.

Epilogo

Ciao amore mio,

I'm thinking of you all the time, but I haven't yet had the courage to write. We are doing OK in general; Pippo likes to sleep on the granny-squares blanket that you made and is hungrier than ever. I need to fix his *gabbietta* (little cage) so that he can spend time outside, now that the weather is turning toward spring. Eamon is a man now, more or less. He's getting into most of the places he applied (it seems to be between UCLA, Oberlin, and Rice), so big decisions are coming up. I trust his instincts. He knows remarkably well who he is now; it's very different from how it was even two or three years ago. He has your temper though; è *fondamentalmente un siculo* (he is basically Sicilian): stubborn as a mule and very fiery. He's driving all the time now, and is actually not bad at it, although he says I make him nervous. He still hasn't learned how to drive the stick shift, which I knew would happen as soon as I let him get his license on the automatic, but what can I do? *Non è più un minorenne.* (He is no longer a minor.)

Some things I have not been so good at. For example, I forgot
to report to jury duty and was late on the telephone bills. Also,
there was some confusion at the last San Francisco Symphony
Youth Orchestra concert; Eamon forgot to bring his tie, and then
I was late to the concert (don't ask), and so he had to borrow his
neckwear. But it worked out in the end. I'm also not vacuuming
as much as you would like, I have to admit, and I haven't been
able to muster any enthusiasm for cooking, as it reminds me too
much of you. We also managed to lose the TV remote, which
I'm sure you would have found instantly. Eamon and I haven't
been able to locate it for weeks. I'll have to do the taxes this year
also; wish me luck, amore. As you know all too well, it's not
really my forte.

On a positive note, I don't forget to eat very often, and I'm
using the juicer to consume the stuff that comes in our produce
box. It's still addressed to you, as are many other things. Do you
think I should bother changing that? Also, the laundry is always
done, the sheets are clean, and the dishes are washed. What about
all the stuff in the bathroom? Your razors are still there; I can't
really bear to throw them out. Remember how much you liked the
Venus when it first came out? Do you think I should clean out the
bathroom? Eamon's bath toys are still hanging in the shower; but
they remind me so much of us, I can't imagine taking them down.
Perhaps I've become the curator of the museum of Emanuela,
Eamon, and Dylan: not, after all, the worst job in the world.

Exercising helps. You would say, *stai esagerando con la corsa*
(you're exaggerating with the running), but it makes me feel
closer to you when I'm out on the trails. I wear your *angelo
prottetore* (guardian angel) and the *pesci* (fish); I'll never take them
off. As you see, I've been trying to write down our story. There
is so much I don't remember clearly, and I'm sure there are a

bunch of mistakes that you would have caught. Still, I think it's turning out pretty well; Donatella has been helping me with the Italian, so I don't make too many egregious errors there, and I would like to have something to give to Eamon before he leaves. I particularly want to try to explain who we were before we became his parents. More than anything I want him to know how madly in love we were; parts of it are even mildly racy. I hope you don't get offended, but I couldn't present us as if we were a couple of enamored saints. How I would love to go over with you again those first few months, that traveling back and forth from Milan to Rome, and the first apartments. Did I at least get the sense of it, even if some of the dates and details are wrong? Did you feel the same way? What was it really like for you? I'm trying to imagine, but I'm trapped in my own perspective, as it were, and I don't have the literary abilities to really transcend that.

Our friends have been amazing; I've got enough gift certificates to eat out every day for the next year, and people are constantly inviting us to dinner or for walks, or just sending beautiful supportive messages. In general, they seem to be very worried about us getting enough food; but we are very well supplied on that front.

I finally took Eamon to the dentist, and everything seems OK, although he needs to have a wisdom tooth extraction, so I'll need to figure that out. I should probably make a doctor's appointment for myself soon as well.

I imagine that you are spending a lot of time with Nonna Angiola, and perhaps Nonno Gigi as well, whom I wish I had met. Do you remember the story you told about the pigeon that came into the apartment on Via Savoia the day after Nonno Gigi's death and walked straight into the bedroom to check on Nonna Angiola? Can you tell Nonna Angiola that I tried my best to *farti felice* (make you happy)? She will know what you're talking about. Also, can you check in on us occasionally? Perhaps you can come as a pigeon or, better yet, a quail, although there aren't very many around here. Do you remember when our cat Julius came back as a slug? I'm sure you will choose *una creatura più bella* (a more beautiful creature), but whatever it is we will know it when we see it. I confess that I may read Elena Ferrante now, even though I know you thought it would be a waste of my time. I'm trying to read more fiction these days, mostly so that I can become a better writer, which seems like the only way I can reach across this divide back to you.

Abbi pazienza, amore (Be patient, my love). Remember that even when I sometimes make decisions that you would have disagreed with, I'm thinking about what you would have thought of them. I'm trying so hard, amore; *sappi soltanto che sto facendo il mio meglio* (know only that I'm doing my best).

A presto, amore. Ti abbraccio forte forte, e penso sempre a te.

Il tuo devoto marito,
Dylan